ILLUMINATION

ILLUMINATION
The Saga of a Spiritual Master

Pir Vilayat Inayat Khan
by Mikhail Horowitz

Sacred Spirit Music

Published by Sacred Spirit Music
5 Abode Rd New Lebanon NY 12125

ISBN-13: 978-1-7321029-0-3

To Taj
who pointed the way and was always
there to help me take the next step.

PREFACE

Pir Vilayat was one of the greatest spiritual masters of the 20th century but much of his story has never been told. His life and what it was like to be with him make an extraordinary story that deserves to be known. My hope is that what follows will help to make him more present, especially for those who were not able to meet him in person.

Pir Vilayat was not one to talk about himself. Many of his stories were told to illustrate his teachings, and the details varied with the telling. His own recollections were given when the inspiration came to him. I was lucky enough to be with him for thirty five years and was able to save many of those inspirations for posterity.

Pir Vilayat was not given to explaining why he did things. To understand this one must know more about who he was, and what made him that way. I have tried to do this to the best of my ability. Hopefully some of these insights will be as useful to other on the spiritual seekers, as they have been to me. It also helps, as he said, "To see oneself in another oneself."

Some of what follows comes from his family or others who were close to him, but my job recording his talks allowed me to travel with him a great deal, and thus to spend more time with him than most. He was not just my teacher but my friend. Preserving his teachings and the music he collected became my mission in life. Much of what I have written was based on the times we spent together. Where possible, I have tried to let him tell his story in his own words. He was careful to avoid saying things that could hurt or embarrass others and I have tried to follow his example.

When I thought it best, I have altered sequences and made small changes in quotations to make them more readable or comprehensible. Many of these were taken from unreleased tapes some of which were made into CDs and may one day hopefully be available. However, many treasures are buried in the thousands of transcripts and recordings we have of him. I have selected some of the finest, as they deserve to be better known and saved for posterity.

Most of the other quotations are from unpublished writings, including, *The Retreat Manual*, and *The Message* magazine series which are presently unavailable as well as his *Keeping in Touch* news letters which are still available on line.

The mistakes and errors herein are all mine. I make no pretense of being a scholar. Thus I have seen fit to pick and choose what I thought best. My hope has always been to tell his story as he would have liked it told, and to include what he would have wanted to pass on to posterity.

I owe a deep debt of thanks to Professor Donald Sharif Graham who collected so many of Pir Vilayat's words and corrected many of my mistakes, as well as to Atum O'Kane to whom I owe much of my understanding of Pir Vilayat and his teachings. Many thanks are also due to Kaivan Plesken who spent untold hours collecting the photographs. And lastly especial thanks to Clare Rosenfield whose generous help and support made it all possible.

Mikhail Horowitz, November 2018

TABLE OF CONTENTS

Chapter 1
THE EARLY YEARS

We are all on a great journey. It's like the horizon, the further you advance, the further you realize that what you thought you saw recedes, and the truth lies further and further away; you realize that you have to be able to wreck your systems on the rock of truth, know how to walk into unknown lands without fear, how to trust beyond all proof. You know who is journeying; it is God who is journeying.
— Pir Vilayat Inayat Khan, *The Great Journey*

Vilayat's father, Hazrat Inayat Khan, was called *Murshid*, which means guide. *Hazrat* is a term of respect. *Inayat* means kindness. More formally, he was called *Pir-o-Murshid*, which was his title as a Sufi teacher and head of the organization he founded. *Pir* is, likewise, a title, meaning elder, which usually refers to the head of an order or a Sufi lineage holder. He was part of a lineage of Sufi masters, the Chishtiyya, or Chishtis as they are called in the West. Pir Vilayat himself was born during World War I. Here are some of his early memories:

I still remember being carried in my father's arms while he sang to me when I was slow to fall asleep. Of course, I avoided falling asleep in order to get him to carry me longer. There were other events I remember clearly, events which took place before I was two. I also remember being pushed in a pram through the streets of London, and that I stayed in the house of Mr. and Mrs. Best while my brother Hidayat was born. I could not have been more than 14 months old at that time. I remember being pushed down to the bomb shelter, when the German Zeppelins were floating over London. I still remember, the sound of the bugles announcing the all clear. There were some lyrics sung then, *All clear, flown away, far away, far away to Germany.*

Pir Vilayat's father was born in 1882 and grew up in Baroda, India. His mother was an American named Ora Ray Baker whom his father met on his first trip to America in 1911.

Inayat Khan was a musician and met her while giving musical lessons in New York. They fell deeply in love. Her older half-brother, who was also her guardian, was unfortunately deeply opposed to her marrying an Indian. In the end she had to elope to England where she married Inayat in 1913. She was twenty-one at the time. Inayat called her Amina Begum, a term of respect. That year they traveled to France and then Russia, where he gave musical performances, playing the vina to receptive audiences. It was there that their first child, Noor-un-Nisa, was born, on New Year's in 1914 before the start of the world war.

As war was about to start they were then forced to return hurriedly to England where they lived until 1920. Vilayat was their second child; he was born on June 19, 1916.

In 1920 Inayat decided to move the family to France. He had created an organization to assist him in his work in England, but there were many problems and personality conflicts. He was a great teacher but had been trained as a musician and knew little about organization. The organization he had created had begun to try to control its creator. To move the family, with very young children, was a drastic choice. The children of course were too young to understand any of the reasons for this radical change.

One of Vilayat's first memories from those times was being seasick on the trip across the Channel. The family was leaving behind a secure situation for an uncertain future. There was barely enough money for food. By then there were four children: Vilayat's six year old sister Noor-un-Nisa, three year old Hidayat, and, youngest of all, one year old Khair-un-Nisa or Claire. None of them even spoke French and there were few French students to help them. It must have been an awful time for the family. Murshid was often away giving talks to bring in funds for their support.

They first lived in a house where Charles de Gaulle Airport would later be built. Within a year they moved again to Wissous. Orly Airport is near there now. Here Vilayat's father began the tradition of holding a summer school, where his students could gather and spend more time with him. He also began to travel to more countries. He found more interest in his teachings in Holland than in France; there he also gave initiation to a number of students who were to help him for the rest of his life.

One of his first trips was to Geneva. He had actually wanted to move the family there, but his wife felt that another move so far from England and where they did not know the language would be too much. He went there purely on intuition, without knowing why, without even the money for food. It was to be a supreme test of faith. Sitting on a bench beside the Lake Geneva, he received the guidance to start the headquarters of the Sufi Movement there, which is what he was able to do. It could not have been coincidence that the League of Nations was also transferred from London to Geneva at just that time. One wonders, if he had been able to live and spend more time there, what could have been the result of his influence on subsequent events.

Everything began to improve for the family when one of his students bought a house for them in Suresnes, outside of Paris. Inayat named the house Fazal Manzil, which means house of blessing. It had been bought for them by a Dutch mureed (student), Mrs. N. Egeling, this is an account that Vilayat wrote about those early years:

> I also remember what for us children was a grueling crossing of the English Channel at the age of four. I still remember the hotel room in the French harbor and talking to my father there. I have a clear memory of the house in the small village called Tremblaye where the family stayed from 1920 to 1921.
>
> There was a stuffed eagle on the wall, which kindled my dreams that later came true when I flew eagles, and I can still recall Murshid sitting at his ease and talking with mureeds.
>
> This was in our next house in Wissous also near Paris. There was a wheat field nearby where he would walk with our mother at sunset. Next I can remember the first days in Fazal Manzil our new house. It was still rural then; the drivers would call out 'Allez yup! Allez yup!' Urging their horses pulling carriages on Rue de La Tuilerie.
>
> At first there was no furniture at all, then Baroness d'Eichthal gave us the wonderful leather chairs which are still there now.

Father and mother could sit on them when they ate. I sometime sat on his lap and could pull his beard.

Mrs. Egeling had been a member of the Theosophical Society and she had read about masters from the East for years. When she first saw Murshid she said, "He is the one!" She offered what little money she had and came to live with them and became sort of a grandmother for the family. Pir said "at that point things started to grow."

Fazal Manzil has become so deeply associated with Hazrat Inayat Khan that it is surprising to know that he was only there part of the year during the final five years of his life. He died prematurely at age forty four. During the summer he taught at the Summer School. Students would come from many countries then.

The main entrance to the house was up a series of steps to the main floor where there was a drawing room, and a room where Fazl Mai kept her things. The children were not allowed to go in there.

The ground floor in later years would be used by Hidayat. In the back part of the house facing the garden there was an enclosed porch. Also facing the garden another smaller room. In it were a number of wooden chairs from India, a table, a small Buddha, a beggars bowl, his prayer beads, and his vina. It was called the "Oriental room," as almost everything there came from the East. This was where Murshid held his interviews.

Claire remembers Mrs. Egeling, or Fazl Mai (God's Blessing) as Inayat called her, as being quite strict. The children were told to be silent much of the time at home. They were not allowed in the room where she kept her things. Vilayat, who rarely spoke of her, would only say that she was "a sweet old lady." She had a harmonium which Inayat would sometimes play when he sang. Claire recounted in her book *We Rubies Four* that she and Hidayat were always mischievous, Noor was kind and helpful and Vilayat rather dreamy.

Much of the year Inayat Khan had to travel giving talks and when possible, and hopefully starting Sufi centers if and when he could find someone up to leading them. He taught in Suresnes only during the summer but much of the rest of the year he was away. He was badly missed, and his absence was especially hard on their mother. The whole family revolved around him and naturally, everyone eagerly awaited his return.

Pir Vilayat remembered those times this way:

> Many children used to play in the field opposite Fazal Manzil, Dutch children, French children, English, German, Swedish, Italian; I was among them.
>
> We spoke the language that children of all lands know so well to make themselves readily understood, peering through the high grass at that mighty figure descending the front steps, opening the gate, crossing the road and wending his way along the narrow path leading to the lecture hall, walking with such majesty. We hid in the grass in wonderment! He could not possibly be my daddy or that of my brothers and sisters! No, he was the father of us all, young or old, the grand patriarch around whom all our lives and beings revolved. Later it became clear he had made a little spot on earth a paradise by his presence.

> When we were children we established a little court beneath the steps. If any child did anything wrong, then the court was convened and Murshid was the judge. We had to own up to what we had done wrong and then we ourselves had to decide what punishment we were going to inflict upon ourselves. The punishment that Murshid gave us was always much less than what we had inflicted upon ourselves. His punishment, which generally consisted in running around the garden three times or something like that, was a form of compassion. The worst punishment was to stand in a corner and not turn around. The important thing was that we ourselves felt that we had to do something to compensate for what we had done; it came from us instead of him, and he taught us to accept blame instead of putting it on others.

> I remember my school time in Suresnes, not speaking any French. The children had never seen a boy with such bronzed skin, with a rather dreamy disposition. They used to pounce on me and beat me up, and I would return home in tears. Murshid said, "Show that you are stronger than they. Catch the most aggressive boy and pin him to the floor until he gives in." I followed his advice, and as a consequence they carried me round in triumph. From that day I was the most popular boy in the class.

Especially in those days, people used to tell a child to do this or do that. Murshid always used to say why. You know how important that is in fact. He took the trouble to tell us. Even when there was a hurry he would say why, although once he said, "I have to be brief because there is not much time."

And I remember him once saying, Well, Vilayat, you could not understand. But as soon as you are old enough to understand, then I will tell you why. That was wonderful, because I was used to him always telling me why, and I knew that the only reason he couldn't say it this time was because I wasn't old enough to understand. This gave us confidence that he would never tell anyone to follow him blindly. That was a policy I have followed all my life: never tell people what to do. In the case of the Murshid, it is because by telling people what to do you are taking away their sense of responsibility and making them into puppets. He could always see exactly what the issue of the problem was, and nevertheless, out of respect for you, he always refrained from telling you what to do.

Establishing and maintaining rhythm was very important for Inayat Khan. There was a regular routine in the house. Early every morning, he did his practices which included exercises and breathing practices. After breakfast, he would accompany himself on the piano or vina and sing. Then, when summer school was in session, he would give interviews for two hours or more. In the afternoons he would give lectures, classes, and occasionally initiations. If there was time he might do some dictation. At the end of day, he would gather the family together and they recited the prayers, *saum*, *salat*, and *khatum*. Then they would sit cross-legged on the floor and sing the dhikr[1]. In this way Vilayat was trained in music and in the importance of maintaining a daily rhythm.

All the family got musical training. At first of course it was Indian music. He also taught them the Western scales, but it was years before they could hear their first Western music, as there was no radio and phonographs were rare then. Hidayat wrote how after hearing his first concert, a Beethoven concerto, he begged his father to get a violin, which both he and Vilayat learned to play. Noor-un-Nisa, the oldest of the four children, and their mother played the tamboura and harp, with which they accompanied the sung dhikrs at times. Their father called the boys "Pirzade" or "Murshidzade," which meant Murshid's son. Instead of reprimanding them he would say, "Have you behaved today like the son of a Murshid?" It was much more effective than scolding.

---

[1] dhikr, often pronounced 'zikr', is an Arabic mantra: 'La illaha illa 'llah hu.'

During summer school he used to call to all the children in the garden of Fazal Manzil, where he told them stories about the lives of the prophets of all the religions. What he was teaching was what would become training for future generations. As Pir Vilayat remembered:

> His time was always taken up, there were always mureeds. He generally slept just about four hours a night, and when he wasn't giving interviews or talks he was meditating. I used sometimes to knock on the door of the Oriental Room, but he would be meditating, so I didn't want to disturb him.
>
> I remember that on occasion I took it upon myself to walk into the room and sit in a little corner quietly and watch him repeat the dhikr or a wazifa. It is almost impossible to convey what I was experiencing in those moments: the whole room was absolutely filled with power. Murshid used to do his practices very internally, so that you could hardly hear the words. It was almost like a whisper: the power came from within.

One day he surprised them and appeared with a driver's license. He had secretly been taking driving lessons. It was rumored that Henry Ford who was so impressed on meeting him, was responsible for getting him a car. He drove just as slowly as he walked. When cars behind him would honk, he would stop, bow to them, and continue on at the same sedate pace. When Inayat went out he always wore a cassock like long black cloak, and his majestic high topi on his head. He carried a walking stick with a fine silver handle. The neighbors believed him to be some kind of Indian noble and called him "Le Grand Seigneur."

Here is Pir Vilayat's description of him:

> We could see him emerging and walking down the steps like a king. In fact, the first thing that impressed us most was the majesty of his being: he walked down with very slow, majestic steps, like a powerful elephant. As he walked, he seemed to be carrying the whole world on his back, and we lay absolutely spellbound by all that was coming through him.
>
> Our lives turned around this great being, when my little companions spoke of their papas, I thought very strange, I don't have a papa, he is the grandfather of us all. He must have been forty-two years old at that time. Now, of course, we were discovering other aspects we hadn't seen before. We were discovering power, a power that was so great that it seemed it could remove mountains. And yet it was a power that one could never be afraid of. Power can be very frightening, but here was a power that was full of kindness. Of course, we as children learned to respect his being because of what he was, so that at no time did he ever have to affirm his power. But it was there, and when we were children, that was what disciplined us.

Pir Vilayat rarely spoke of his mother. There were so many painful memories; however, here is one account that he wrote:

> My memories of my mother give rise to such deep feelings in me. She was so beautiful, so gentle, so filled with selflessness, a wonderful being. She was a product of the best of America. Sensitive, reserved, dignified, and at the same time lively and free.
>
> Reading my father's letters to her and hers to him, my heart was bursting. It was a desperate romance of Romeo and Juliet intensity. Her half-brother was Doctor Bernard, a physician who became quite proficient in yoga. As President of the Tantric Yoga Order he invited my father to teach music in New York. There he met my mother. It was love at first sight. Dr Bernard was fascinated by the East but definitely drew the line at his half-sister, who was to become my mother, marrying an Easterner. He obstructed their correspondence. In the end my mother fled in a dramatic elopement to London so she could marry him at last. Their first child Noor was born in Moscow on January 1,

1914.

Looking back, I can clearly see now scenes of mureeds pushing her aside to be closer to Murshid. Because she was naturally soft and accommodating, she withdrew with a wounded heart. I remembered how she carried heavy buckets of coal up stairs throughout the day to keep the stoves going in this big house.

It was only during the summer months that they could count on his staying in Suresnes. This was the time when the children could see the most of him. In the first years classes were given in the garden unless it was raining. In general there were seventy to eighty people attending at any one time.

Hazrat Inayat Khan's brothers were much more traditional and could never accept the fact that he had married a modern American woman, although they themselves took Dutch wives, apart from Ali Khan (his cousin) who never married. Initially they all lived in the same house. Perhaps in part because of this, Vilayat's mother assumed the role of a traditional Indian wife. We do not know whether Inayat urged this on her, but perhaps she herself felt more comfortable in this role. She wore robes and was referred to as Amina Begum. In the traditional Muslim culture, the wife would never be seen without her husband or another male family member and Inayat was away much of the time. After the move to France they lived mostly in Holland where they lived with their Dutch wives, however, they came to Suresnes during the Summer School. Vilayat had good memories of his uncle Maheboob from this time.

By 1925 classes could be given in the newly built lecture hall across the road or in the garden. Sometimes there were leaders and a mureed or two at lunch. Their father always sat at the head of the long table, their mother facing him at the other end. Then the children had a table of their own. Most often Sharifa Goodenough would be there. She would speak Persian with their father since her mother was a noble Persian. She was very strict with the children, telling them not to talk as Murshid liked to keep the house as silent as possible. The best times for the children were Sundays, when their father did not give classes and they could spend time with him. Each day they were given a subject for concentration such as patience, tolerance, forgiveness, kindness or ·

humility. They looked forward to being able to tell him that they had actually done it and how.

Pir-o-Murshid initiated a total of four women as Murshidas, this was the highest rank next to that of the Pir, unheard of at that time for Sufis, and still very rare. The first was an American women Ada Martin, Fazl Mai Egeling who was Dutch, Sophia Saintsbury Green, and Sharifa Goodenough who were English. He was closest to Murshida Goodenough who spoke Persian and had studied Sufism before she met him. She was aristocratic but not very outgoing or friendly.

More students came to hear Murshid give teachings during the summer months. Many had originally been part of the Theosophical Society in England or Holland. In those days Suresnes was more like a village than the suburb it has become. Some of the wealthy students built houses nearby. After a few years a nearby house for mureeds with nineteen rooms was acquired. At that time, there was a large field across the street where their father loved to walk and the children could play. That was where the lecture hall was being built. The Suresnes Summer School was followed in September by an additional two-week Summer School, hosted by Baron Sirdar and Saida van Tuyll at their villa in Katwijk-aan-Zee, a scenic seaside village in the Netherlands near Leiden.

Pir-o-Murshid often sat under an apricot tree in the garden where he would talk with his students.

Here is Pir Vilayat's description:

I remember how Murshid sat under a tree in the garden, in deep meditation, and then he would speak to a circle of mureeds about life in the angelic spheres before and after life on earth. We children were not allowed to attend the lectures. But I do remember slipping by the sentinels and edging my way into the lecture hall. I will never forget the sacredness pervading the hall as his hallowed figure entered and filled the space with his magnetism. One sensed such love and reverence emanating from the mureeds. Nor will

I ever forget the sacredness emerging from his voice as he said, "Beloved ones of God."

I was present when Murshid had the inspiration of the Universal Worship and the prayers, which, in fact, came together. We were children, and as with all children, we liked to climb into our parents' bed in the morning and cuddle and pull on Murshid's beard. But that morning our mother said, "No, you can't come in the room now because Murshid is in a special state and he must be left at peace. Naturally we were extremely curious to see Murshid in a special state, and so we kept loitering around so that if there were a slight opening of the door we would be able to see what was happening. Later we did manage to come inside. Murshid was in a very, very high state, and of course we felt that something very important, very cosmic was happening, although we did not know what it was.

Later, not long afterward, the Universal Worship was celebrated in the drawing room of Fazal Manzil. Murshid sat in one of the leather chairs at one side of the altar, and a cherag sat on the other side. There was the lighting of the candles, the reading of the scriptures, and so on, but of course the presence of Murshid gave it such a very powerful atmosphere. He said a few words at the end and he gave the blessing. That of course was a great moment, when he gave the blessing.

My mother later said that the whole structure of the Universal Worship was given as a revelation. This is the way of worship for our time; it replaces the ways that were given in the past.

There was a sense of impending tragedy that last year, 1926. For some time Murshid had expressed his intention to visit India, or was it to return to India? My mother was continually in tears. Murshida Fazl Mai was very concerned. Noor dreamt that the baker had flown off in a plane, never to return again. When she told the dream to Murshid there were tears in his eyes. Little did we realize at that time that maybe he was foreseeing what would happen to her in World War II.

I remember once when Murshid was very ill, also in 1926, and he had a high fever. I went into the Oriental Room, and he really wasn't up to speaking, but I could hear him repeating, very softly, zikr.

I had a dream that he had left on the train. We generally would have accompanied him, and that my brother and sisters had left to accompany him and I had missed it. And so I was in a terrible state in my sleep because somehow there was a feeling that I picked up that Pir-o-Murshid would not come back after his trip to India. And this was my last opportunity. I was in a situation of shock. So I screamed in my sleep. And I was in the room next to my father and mother. I heard his voice saying, "Bhaijan (that means dear brother) it's all right. Don't worry." And then I went back to sleep.

The next day, that last Sunday in August 1926, knowing that Murshid did not attend the services anymore, this being the only time he was not engaged in either lectures or interviews, I waited until everyone had left and gingerly knocked at the door of the Oriental Room. This was my one chance of talking to him alone. This time when I knocked at the door, everyone had left and Murshid was alone, as it was during the Universal Worship service.

As I knocked at the door of the Oriental Room, I remembered the dream. So he said, "Come in, my son." He was looking out the window. And there was my mother with the three children taking them to the Universal Worship. He was very silent and pensive. He said, "I hope that you will marry someone like your mother." In his wisdom, he seized this opportunity to speak of the big choices

I would have to make in my life. We sat on the seat and he said, "If there is a war what will you do?" I said, "I don't want to fight. I don't want to kill." He said, "Yes, you can fight without killing. But if you are eating the bread of a country, you owe your loyalty to the people of that country." And so that was a message for my participation in the war and that of Noor.

I said, "Abba, why do you not go to the Universal Worship?" And he said, "This is time for the mureeds to look after themselves." Then I had a terrible shock because it seemed to confirm that he wouldn't come back. So then I said, "But they would never be able to continue without you." Then he looked very sad and he said, "Well, they will have to." There was a long moment of silence, and then he said, "Yes, there are going to be very difficult times. People are going to fight against each other. All of the evil in the hearts of people will come up again." And then he made this remark, "You see, just giving the lectures and meetings and meditations was wonderful. The problem was organization."

All of a sudden I could feel, in a way, the heartbreak. "If I had stayed in the East," he said, "I would have been sitting under a tree next to the Ganges, and people would have come and bowed their heads in the dust and I could have given them blessings." He looked at my shoes and said, "You will follow in my footsteps. But you will have to prepare yourself. You will meet with trials and have to grow acquainted with the ways of the world."

There was a ceremony in the field across the road from Fazal Manzil, where Murshid had hoped the *Universel*, a temple symbolizing the underlying unity of the great religions, would be built. Murshid laid its foundation stone.

In preparing the ceremony his mureeds drew a circle on the ground and marked a point in the middle where Murshid should stand. They did not know that in mystic traditions the circle is the symbol for endlessness. To be enclosed in endlessness means that he passes into the hereafter. Murshid hesitated, then reluctantly stepped into it. Vilayat remembers that the mood was somber at what had been planned as a festive occasion.

On September 13th, 1926, Inayat left for India. He had wanted to go for a year, although we do not know why, but perhaps it was in the hope of curing an illness which the doctors in France could not treat, possibly a form of walking pneumonia. The trip was kept secret; few outside of the family knew that he was going. One wonders why it had to be kept secret? That was to cause many problems.

Actually Inayat had wanted to go to India in 1925 but had been dissuaded from doing so by his brother Maheboob. The family was afraid that he might not return. Instead he went to America where he stayed away for seven months, but accomplished little. Samuel Lewis who was to become Murshid Sam, reported that at that time Inayat seemed bitterly disappointed and said, "How many loyal mureeds do you think I have?" " I wish I had twenty! I wish I had ten! I wish I had five loyal mureeds! Five loyal mureeds. I have not as many loyal mureeds as I have fingers on one hand." This would seem to indicate that he felt that his mission to the West had been a failure.

Although there had been many premonitions, no one could have been prepared for the news that he had died in India. Not that they could ever really be prepared for such a loss. He had been the mainstay of their whole world. It was not even clear why he had died. He traveled with his Dutch secretary Kismet Stam. They visited many places and she said that he saw doctors wherever they went. The main biography we have of him states, "After a few busy months traveling and lecturing, he passed away after a short illness in Delhi on February 5, 1927." When he died the room was filled with the scent of roses. He was only forty-four years old. Pir Vilayat remembered that time thus:

> I was very young when Hazrat Inayat Khan passed away; I was ten years old. I remember receiving the telegram. We couldn't believe it. It was as if our whole world had been shattered, had come to an end. We didn't think it was possible to live without him. We couldn't believe that we wouldn't see him again. It was totally unacceptable.

There is a mystery about how he could leave with so many things undone. The family was not even clear about why he had gone. There was no one else who could possibly fill the void that he had left. The mureeds were confused. Murshid's brothers were living in Holland most of the time and were not close to the family. Unfortunately, he gave no clear instructions as to who he wanted to head the Order, and how the work was to continue in case of his absence. Everyone assumed that he wanted Vilayat to be his successor, but he was only ten at that time.

One possibility was that the thought of his death at this time was just too painful for Inayat Khan to contemplate or openly discuss with the family. His wife was passionately opposed to her son having to shoulder his father's role, knowing all too well the pain and suffering which it entailed. Thus, it was quite possible that in deference to her, Inayat put off declaring his successor.

Vilayat always believed that his father had put his own name after his on the *silsilla* of Chishti lineage holders, which was placed underneath the cornerstone of the Universel and which mysteriously disappeared. However, in neglecting the essential task of making his choice known publicly, he created a void which it seemed negative forces came to fill. The unforeseen consequences would multiply over time and greatly added to the burdens Vilayat would have to carry in the future.

Chapter 2
LIFE WITHOUT MURSHID

When you go through the dark night of the soul you do not have anything on which to cleave. Nobody can help you and all of those things onto which you are holding fail you.

The challenge of our lives includes both victory and despair. You have to go through a breakdown before you can reach a breakthrough.

— PIR VILAYAT INAYAT KHAN

If the move to France had been difficult for the family, the period that followed Inayat's death became much worse. Their mother broke down completely. She had always been frail, but now she would remain essentially bedridden for most of the next twelve years. Vilayat was only ten, and his brother Hidayat and sister Claire even younger. What happened was that twelve year old Noor-un-Nisa was forced into the role of their "little mother" in Vilayat's words. She was much too young to fulfill this role. The whole experience was to leave deep wounds on them all.

There was no agreement as to who was to head the Sufi Movement or how the work was to be continued. No provision had been made to train an interim successor, nor was there any agreement on who this should be. Murshida Goodenough had been the closest to Inayat. Her whole life revolved around him and the guidance he gave her. The strain of her sudden loss was too much, and she broke down and required hospitalization, from which she never fully recovered.

After two years, the controversial choice was made by the senior leadership of the Movement to select the older of Murshid's brothers, Maheboob Khan. He was given the title Shaikh-ul-Mashaikh (Sheikh of Sheikhs) rather than Pir. A number of senior leaders disagreed with this decision. He had neither the training nor the higher initiation required for this role. Without the guiding inspiration that Inayat Khan had always given there was much conflict within the organization and the work that he had started suffered as a result. It quickly became clear just how much he had left unfinished.

Without Inayat Khan's income the family was almost totally dependent on Fazl Mai Egeling for financial support. Her devotion had been to him. Pir Vilayat once told us how his father had advised her about investments and he was always right, but now he was gone. She was still living with them, but without their father's income funds were short. Even the rights to his books had been signed over to the Sufi Movement instead of the family. With their mother bedridden everything was very difficult. In some ways the period of mourning never ended. The curtains in the house were drawn and stayed that way. One of his uncles told young Vilayat, "You should never laugh again." Noor was totally devoted to their mother who remained deeply depressed. Instead of a house filled with cheer and laughter that might have lightened her mood, everyone tried to shield and protect her. This continued until the German invasion forced them to flee.

After a number of months the family traveled to Inayat's grave site. Claire remembers Noor saying, "He is not there." Fazl Mai had financed the venture, which included a visit to the Taj Mahal and other places. It was not a happy trip. Their mother was still often crying with Noor trying her best to comfort her. The uncles were not close to them, and they did not travel together.

From the time she was little, Noor had a quiet sweetness. She was always kind and considerate, in fact almost to the point of being saintly; her life was devoted to serving others. As he grew older, Vilayat gradually was able to shoulder more responsibilities for the family. In the end he would become a pillar of strength on whom they could all rely.

Many of the mureeds left, including some of the key organizers. Subsequently neither Vilayat nor the others spoke or wrote of these awful years. However, he did say that he was helped by a Catholic teacher who was tutoring him in math and who had helped inspire his faith. Vilayat said, "He explained how you must be able to believe, even when the facts seem to prove the opposite."

Thanks to their father they had their love of music to sustain them. It was one of the finest gifts they inherited from him. Noor had her harp and both boys played the violin.

They could all play the piano as well. Vilayat switched to the cello in time. Hidayat went on to study composition and music was to remain a great love for him. He composed a number of fine classical pieces. Vilayat's music, which he loved deeply, helped sustain him through these difficult times. He wrote:

> As a young man, my mother tried to save me from having to undergo all the hardships that my father underwent. And so she encouraged me to be a musician as well as my brother and sisters. All four of us children studied at the École Normale de Musique at its heyday as the leading music school of its time — with Nadia Boulanger, Cortot, Thibaut, Casals, Maria Landowska, Stravinsky, and Paul Dukas.
>
> We attended the musical courses of the world's virtuosos and went through the most proficient training of the time. Noor studied the harp, I the cello with Maurice Eisenberg; Hidayat with Mr. Roth of the Lerner Quartet; and Claire the piano. We studied composition with Nadia Boulanger, the teacher of teachers. Stravinsky used to grace the classes with his presence. I spent the summer in San Vicente in Spain, taking lessons from Maurice Eisenberg and listening to Pablo Casals practicing in his villa by the sea.

Nadia Boulanger was a great teacher, and clearly had the deepest impact on Vilayat of any of his music teachers. It was from her that he began to learn many of his own teaching skills. From her he would also learn the art of teaching teachers. With her inspiration he also wrote a number of compositions which he played on the piano.

Claire remembered that at age fifteen Vilayat had started collecting books on Sufism, and he had so many he had to spread them out on the dining room table. He gave his first class on his father's teachings when he was sixteen. He wrote a drama fittingly called *The Light of Truth* since light and truth remained of overriding importance for him the rest of his life. He had some of his father's teachings, but many were transcriptions of his talks in shorthand notes which he could not read.

In 1934, when he was 18, Vilayat traveled with Noor to the south of France, crossed the Pyrenees, and toured Spain. He began to learn Spanish, as it was his habit of learning the language in each country where he spent time. They visited Maurice Eisenberg, who took them to see Pablo Casals who lived nearby. Vilayat managed to get some private lessons with Casals. Subsequently, he went there every summer and attended the Masters Classes he gave. This was also the period that Casals did his great recordings of the Bach cello suites, which have never been surpassed. Pir Vilayat spoke of him as being very stern and a very strict teacher. Vilayat attributed his rich tone to what he learned from him. He always played from the heart; what mattered was the emotions that he could convey. Once he gave up studying music, there was no time to practice and so mistakes were inevitable, but that would never stop him for playing for us during the music camps he would give.

The next summer Noor and Vilayat went to Italy, where they attended a music festival in Venice. They were enthralled by what they heard in the Basilica San Marco where Claudio Monteverdi had conducted his great choral works, including the *Vespers of 1610*, which he wrote to be performed in the special acoustics of the cathedral's two choir lofts.

Many years later during sacred moments of retreats Pir would play recordings of Gabrielli and Monteverdi which had been performed in the same Basilica. This was the first time most of us had heard such sublime music. I can still remember the impact it when I first heard it; I never knew such beauty and exaltation existed! It was the performances that made all the difference. These were rare recordings that Vilayat had collected over the years, with performances which gave these works the truly sacred character they deserved. Few indeed were the conductors with the attunement to achieve this.

One of the things that he and Noor shared was their love of music. They also enjoyed riding together. She had a strong connection with Baron and Baroness van Tuyll, two longtime mureeds of their father who lived in a seaside villa in Holland. From time to time she and Vilayat would stay at their house. They had a fine library and thoroughbred horses, which they rode on the hard sand of the beach.

In 1937 the two went to Switzerland, where they stayed for many weeks in a small cabin above Lake Zug, looking out on a panorama of snow clad peaks. This was one of their very happiest times together. It had become a tradition for them to do at least one trip every year to different places in Europe. They shared a spiritual attunement which made for deep empathetic understanding. The bond of love and understanding between them had been cemented by all they had suffered together. She was very sensitive, and as he grew older he could shield her, just as she had helped him in the awful time after their father's death. Jean Fuller, a friend she met in England, says that they were both "highly strung and easily upset," but beneath Noor's gentle manner and sensitivity lay an iron resolve and unbreakable courage. Vilayat appeared to others as headstrong and very determined.

Each was in the process of discovering themselves. Naturally they had both been greatly molded by their father, and shared his ideals. Vilayat had devoted himself to studying his teachings while Noor was less certain of her beliefs. They decided to study Hindi together, as they were losing the little they had known. Their father had spoken it as well as Gujarati with his brothers, but now they rarely saw them.

Noor read widely, especially in Eastern religions, although she was not ready to accept all of her father's ideas uncritically. She tended to be dreamy and rather unworldly, however, she was patient, neat and efficient. She loved to write. She was so excited when the first of her children's stories was published in a French magazine and kept on writing more of these. They generally had symbolic or spiritual meaning. She also wrote a book entitled *Jataka Tales* which was published in 1940. It is a collection of 20 stories of animals resolving difficult situations with compassion and wisdom.

The Summer School, although smaller than in Murshid's times, was still held in Suresnes. Vilayat sometimes gave classes or chaired the meetings. He gave his first gatha class at age sixteen. The lecture hall across the road where Pir-o-Murshid had wanted to build the Universel was still there, but many of the mureeds no longer had houses in the neighborhood.

Murshid's absence was very apparent and he was badly missed. Most of the classes were based on what he had said or written, and everything was done as much as possible just as he had done them.

Vilayat was being pulled in several different directions. While he was drawn to music and meditation, he also had wide-ranging interests spanning religion, philosophy, and science as well. Increasingly he had the conviction that he should follow in his father's footsteps which would mean leading the movement he had founded. He began to wear his father's heart and wings on special occasions.

It was becoming clearer to him that despite his mother's urging he could no longer push aside his destiny. No doubt, as he would say, the pull of the future was stronger than the push of the past. He wrote:

At that particular juncture (in the mid 1930s) I was the father of the family and Noor was the mother. I had been offered an opportunity to go to India to do training amongst the yogis. And somehow, I felt that I would be letting people down, letting my family down by leaving. So I was faced with a very difficult choice. I eventually decided to stay and it was only much later, in fact after the war, that I was able to go to India, and live as a sannyasin in the Himalayas.

When I was eighteen Murshida Fazl Mai reminded me of my father's wish, enjoining me to prepare myself for the great task of having a university education. I remembered pledging myself in the Oriental Room, giving up my beloved music as Murshid had done, and belatedly recommencing my studies.

At that time, I remembered the words of Murshid when he was asked, "What will Vilayat do when he is grown up?" And he said, "He will present the Message to the intellectual world." So I thought well, maybe he wants me to have a real solid education, so I started studying philosophy at the Sorbonne. It was hard uphill work, but it was exciting and challenging to my mind. I was moved by an insatiable curiosity, I needed to know. I thought psychology would be right-on if it included spirituality. At any rate I reasoned that psychology would be incomplete without physiology on the one hand and spirituality on the other. So in addition to philosophy and psychology, I set out to study physics which required advanced mathematics, chemistry, biology, and physiology. Can you imagine that range of subjects?

I spent half of every night standing up at a blackboard to keep from dropping off to sleep. In one hand a cup of coffee and (admittedly) a cigarette in the other. The effort culminated in a thesis for a diploma in psychology, based on psychological factors in neurological reaction time.

Commuting from Paris in 1940 I spent time at Oxford, researching at the Bodleian Library and attending the lectures of Professor H.H. Price. In addition, I attended the classes of comparative religion at the École des Hautes Études, including classes of Professor Massignon, the Sufi Scholar who brought the contribution of al-Hallaj to light.

But I always felt there was something wrong about the wisdom of the world, and as you know, when one is very young one doesn't really see what is wrong with it. It just doesn't feel right. And I had a terrible problem of reconciling what I was learning at the university, which was philosophy, with what Hazrat Inayat Khan was saying. They didn't seem compatible in the least. Now of course, looking back upon it all, it's become very clear how our thinking is based upon logic, and as soon as you see how fallacious logic is, then you're not fooled by it any longer. Most people are fooled by it.

There is an Oxford limerick that defines the philosopher as a blind man in a dark room looking for a black cat that isn't there. At that time, I suppose I was that blind man; I couldn't find the black cat either. Murshid knew all the time that there wasn't a black cat there, because he was endowed with a greater wisdom, the wisdom that sees into the soul. I had planned to work for a doctorate but then the war came, which interrupted everything of course.

It was his great good fortune to have been able to study with Louis Massignon, the saintly professor who was one of the first to bring his deep understanding of Sufism to Western audiences. He fostered Vilayat's deep connection with Mansour Al-Hallaj, which remained a key source of inspiration all of his life.

Each in his own way shared a passionate belief in the need to fight injustice. They both did as much as they could to resist French repression of the Algerian independence movement. Massignon even participated in demonstrations, something almost unheard of for a university professor.

While he was in London Vilayat became a co-leader of the small Sufi center there and began giving talks under the auspices of the Sufi Movement. He was an excellent speaker and thus gained confidence in both his abilities and his understanding of Sufism.

Chapter 3
THE WAR YEARS AND AFTER

*Do not be bewildered if you do not know where you are going, because
the purpose of life is like the horizon. Realize that all you thought proves
itself to be void and all that you had reckoned upon breaks down like a pack
of cards. Do not try to occupy a position that is not yours. Fight the battle of
life with your self first. Mastery consists in never giving in to self-pity. Pain
makes the soul sincere. Wash the feet of those who spit at your face and answer
by kindness and generosity. Turn your temper into the dignity of the one who
is walking above the sea of life.*
— PIR VILAYAT INAYAT KHAN, *THE GREAT JOURNEY*

On a June afternoon in 1940 Noor and Vilayat sat in the living
room of Fazal Manzil debating what to do. The Germans were coming
closer and time was short. Neither had French citizenship. Vilayat with
an English passport might be arrested. Noor had been born in Moscow,
but her father was Indian and her mother American. They did not
have many connections with England. In fact, their sympathies were
with India and Gandhi's fight for Indian independence from British
colonialism. Beyond this, their allegiance was to their father's message
and individual freedom. What could they do under the coming German
occupation? Where to go? How would they live? Should they join the
British army? Fazl Mai had died in 1939, but the funds she had left
them were mostly in Holland, which by that time was under German
occupation. As Pir recounted:

> I remember my conversation with Noor, my sister, when we
> heard the cannons of the Nazis advancing towards the gates of
> Paris. We had to decide whether we were going to stay or not, if
> we were going to participate in the war. None of us wanted to kill.
> Does it mean if one joins the forces, one has to kill? I remember

saying to Noor, supposing that you have a Nazi with a machine
gun and he's about to shoot the hostages and your only chance to
save them is to shoot the Nazi, what do you do? Because we were
evoking Gandhi's nonviolence and I realized that nonviolence is
a general principle but in some cases one really has to intervene.
But then Noor said, "Well yes, but I couldn't kill." And I said,
"Yes, I couldn't kill either." So then we pondered on how could one
participate in the war without killing. At one point I remembered
what my father had said, "If you are eating the bread of a country,
you owe your loyalty to the people of that country." And so that
was a message for my participation in the war. We were both
British citizens and we decided to leave and to join forces with the
English. In the end I didn't quite follow that principle because I
trained as a fighter pilot but that was again the same thing to save
populations of the cities from the bombers. It did mean killing. I
was following that idea of how do you deal with the Nazi.

They managed to convince their mother and Claire to come
with them to England. Hidayat who was married and had children
and decided not to leave the country. Claire narrates how she, her
mother, Noor and Vilayat all fled the German advance jammed into
a little two-seater MG sports car. Hidayat left with his family and
one uncle in another car to the south of France. It was a fearsome
time to travel. Rumors were everywhere but hard news was scarce.
The roads were clogged with panicked humanity fleeing in anything
they could find, they knew not where. German dive bombers
strafing the refugees flew so low that they could see the pilots' faces,
who obviously knew exactly what they were doing. They passed
horrible casualties along the roadsides. This experience resolved
any lingering doubts that Vilayat still had about the necessity of
fighting.

They were able to get as far as Tours and then took a packed
train to Bordeaux. When it arrived, they were not allowed to get off,
as the town was overloaded with refugees and they ended up about
fifty miles away. After five terrible days during which Noor and
Claire were separated from Vilayat and his mother, he managed to
buy a motorcycle and took them one by one to a Belgian freighter
on which they were to sail to England. They were safe at last, it was
June 19th, his birthday.

They heard SOS calls on the ship's radio and warnings of German submarine attacks. However, the sea was calm and they were not attacked. England felt like a haven of peace by comparison, but all too soon it would become a besieged fortress, facing Nazi Germany alone. The army had been evacuated from Dunkirk under German air attack, leaving all its equipment behind.

Luckily Vilayat had friends in Oxford where they could stay at first. After the turmoil they had left behind in France, England seemed strangely peaceful. However, they had only the money they had been able to bring with them, which meant they were really poor and almost totally dependent on the generosity of others. Vilayat and Noor planned to join the armed forces. Claire and their mother found work with the Red Cross which barely provided them with enough to eat. Their mother had never worked before this and she was still quite frail. They had lived such sheltered lives; she had rarely even left the family home all these years. Now they were refugees.

Jean Fuller became a close friend of Noor's at that time. She was a writer and was to tell Noor's story in the book *Madeleine*. She remembers in the days before they knew what Noor was doing that Vilayat told her,

> I have a presentiment that in this life my sister will have to meet the most utter blackness of the world. This is the valley down which she will have to walk alone. I know if I were to prevent her it would be wrong, because it would be interfering with something that is necessary to her evolution, and yet I shudder.

Since Noor's story is well known a brief summary will suffice. She joined the WAAF, the Women's Auxiliary Air Force, mostly because her brother had been accepted for pilot training. However, the fact that she was fluent in French brought her to the notice of the intelligence services. As a result, she was transferred to the Special Operations Executive, the innocuous name for the secret spy service, and underwent intense training in wireless and code transmission, spy craft, and weapons. Despite the doubts of her superiors, she volunteered for assignment in Paris, where few agents lasted more than six weeks. Unknown to her family, she was smuggled into occupied France. All she could tell them was that she had been trained as a radio operator.

Vilayat was to relate her story as follows:

> Noor volunteered for the most dangerous of all positions. A radio operator in Paris. She was given away by a friend of hers, a traitor, to the Nazis for a hundred thousand francs. After her arrest, this shy feminine girl made an attempt to escape from the Gestapo Headquarters in Paris, but was caught, then thrown into a lorry and taken to a prison in Karlsruhe. There she was handcuffed and chained and kept in total isolation for ten months. She was offered everyday a soup made of potato peels that burn the stomach. Finally she was transferred to Dachau, a terrible concentration camp. And she was left practically in the nude I think the whole night. It might have been raining outside. And the *gauleiter* (Nazi guard) kept on kicking her with his heavy boots as she lay on a cement floor in chains, suffering agony from enormous hematomas all over her body. And the next day there she was waiting to be killed. And the *gauleiter* beat her up so badly that she was, as the report says, a bloody mess. Then she was made to kneel and was shot in the head from behind. But she didn't cry. Her last words were, "Vive la liberté."
>
> Apparently, there was still some motion in her body when she was thrown into the oven that is still in Dachau. That was my sister, such a beautiful sensitive person, who wrote children's stories, and played the harp.

Late in the war when the allied armies were sweeping across Germany liberating the concentration camps, Noor came to Jean Fuller in a dream; she was surrounded by a blue light and said, "I am free." When Jean saw Vilayat he said he had dreamed the same thing. Whereas Jean thought it meant that she had been liberated, Vilayat concluded the opposite. He said, "It means she is dead."

Vilayat was had always dreamed that he would some day be able to fly so naturally he joined the air force and went through pilot training. As he had long suspected when the chance finally came he discovered that he passionately loved to fly. He told us how he loved to turn off the engine and glide while hanging upside down.

He related:

At one point, I was trained in the Royal Air Force by a
Battle-of-Britain pilot. Within three lessons, he put me through
the most hair-raising acrobatics. I returned the gauntlet by putting
him into an inverted spin which he said later we were lucky to
come out of. My joy was making a half loop, then turning off
the engine and drifting in the wind amongst the clouds upside
down, hanging on my straps in an open cockpit. Everything stops,
you stop worrying, stop striving, you're not even trying to self
transcend. Here I was at home, set free in the vastness. In fact,
my dearest wish would have been to live up there permanently. I
would exult in the many splendored array of colors in the clouds,
and their evanescent formations and I would turn my plane into
the sun, drinking in its sheer effulgence as I glided upon thin air.

It was too good to last; he was transferred to the British navy,
officially because of poor night vision, but he hinted that the reason was
actually that he kept on taking forbidden risks: he loved to do loops and
fly upside down! At that stage he fancied motorcycles and sports cars.

Speed and danger had quite an attraction for him then.

However, he was destined to spend the rest of the war at sea. This may well have saved his life; mortality rates among fighter pilots were the highest of any service. Nonetheless, the navy was a severe trial. At first he had to serve as a common seaman. He complained in one letter to Noor that his time was spent in such tasks as carrying potato sacks and picking up cigarette butts. The whole experience was a rude awakening for him. In fact, he was so furious that Noor worried he would desert and join the Maquis in France. His time on the lower decks had thrust him into a rough world that he had thus far been shielded from. His life up until then had been lived mostly in the rarified atmospheres of Fazal Manzil and studying music and philosophy.

His deepest need had always been to be free. This was a severe challenge. Overcoming it helped him to develop some of the mastery which became one of his most outstanding qualities. He not only met this challenge, but his background helped him to become a spokesman for the seamen, and thus quite popular on the "lower decks." In the end he was transferred to officer training. One day the captain told him, "You must not have friends among the men." Vilayat responded, "But you even drink with them." "I can afford to," the captain replied. Vilayat understood that he needed to learn how the captain had acquired his authority. Clearly, he was in a perfect situation to learn this. Later he used this to illustrate to us the difference between *Qaher* and *Qadr*, sovereignty as distinct from power.

His training started on land and then moved to a trawler which was doing patrols along the East Coast of England. Next he was sent to a destroyer escorting convoys to the Mediterranean. He had never been drawn to the sea and here he was forced to experience it at its worst. Destroyers were considered the most uncomfortable ships afloat in those rough waters. Gales were frequent and one was always drenched by the frigid spray, the deck itself frequently awash under cold waves. Not for nothing were they called tin cans, rolling and pitching like demented things. Finally he was transferred to minesweeping duties. He still hated it, but at least now he could fight evil, while not taking lives, which was what his father had suggested.

One of his tasks was to search for submarines while on watch duty. This required spotting a periscope, a tiny speck in a vast gray sea, an almost impossible task. However, he explained that this was a first step in learning to use intuition, a vital discovery. It was important training for him in other ways as well.

When the time came, he was part of a mine sweeping flotilla clearing the way for the Normandy invasion, working to disarm some of the thousands of mines strewn along the coast. It was scary dangerous work. He recounted,

> I was ahead of the landing troops. So we were shot up from all sides. I would see my friends, we'd been drinking the night before at a party, and the next day I could see them floating in the water, dead. I knew I was next. We never expected to survive.

He had his own close brush with death in the cold waters of the English Channel. He had never learned to swim and felt like an eternity before he was rescued. This was a searing experience, leaving him with bronchitis and a chronic cough which plagued him the rest of his life.

Following the landing they had to ferry supplies to the beachhead, and then did mine sweeping as far north as Norway. After the war's end he still had to remain in the navy, serving out his enlistment. At his request he was allowed to transfer to India. He did not yet know how Noor had died, but he knew she was not coming back and blamed himself. Although he said that he could never enjoy the sea again, his time in the Royal Navy gave him useful training. There he first learned the importance of commanding the respect and trust of those under him. There was one incident in particular that was most instructive in this way. He had arrived shortly before Indian independence, just when an incipient mutiny had started among native sailors. The situation had turned ugly, when an Indian officer took it on himself to go out in front of them unarmed, with just his commanding presence and well-chosen words; he calmed them and thus was able to save the situation. Here is Pir's account:

> I will never forget what happened to me at the end of the Second World War. I was an officer in the British Navy, in Bombay, of all places, at a time when there was a meeting of the Indian Navy. A whole sea of Indian sailors were coming to attack the British officers in the barracks. The admiral in charge of the barracks, who himself was an Indian, an admiral in the Indian Navy, asked us to stay where we were. Many of the officers wanted to overpower him. We were scared stiff, of course, and the admiral said, "No, let me take over," and he walked out facing the crowd. He faced them and spoke to them for about an hour, and then turned back and walked away. That was one of the most admirable scenes I've ever experienced. It was testing the marvelous authority of that admiral, who had really mastered violence himself and therefore was able to somehow master it in those people. It was an example of the Divine Sovereignty in human form.

On leave from Bombay where he was stationed he traveled to Peshawar where he met a captain who was a falconer. When the eagle landed on Vilayat's outstretched arm, a falconer was born in the young naval officer. He decided to go to Afghanistan where falconry was widely practiced.

Watching eagles there he remembered how, at age seven, he saw an eagle in the Paris zoo and had what he later realized was a *déjà vu*. He now realized that he had seen himself as a Mongol chieftain, with a large bird on his wrist. A little later he saw a stuffed eagle in a museum.

He was transfixed and did not want to leave. Gradually he understood the reasons for what was to become a lifelong passion. When a friend asked him, "Were you really an eagle in a past lifetime?" He answered, "Of course, don't I look like an eagle?" Most falconers flew peregrines, kestrels, or other smaller birds. Vilayat, however, felt particularly drawn to eagles. Not surprisingly, they were also his totem.

Falconry was probably practiced in Europe long before the crusades, but it became a noble sport in Europe when the Crusaders were able to learn the finer points that the Arabs had developed. With their return books on falconry began to be translated into Latin. It was only then that the Franks learned to make hoods to cover the birds' heads, for example. The word in Arabic for these hoods is *burqa*, which is also the robe with which women cover themselves.

Mongols had also been keen falconers. Pir believed that he had inherited this trait along with his Mongol blood. Over the years he had flown many different birds: falcons, hawks, and even a buzzard. But his preference had always been for eagles. Golden Eagles were traditionally reserved for the highest nobility. Eagles were the most challenging, especially if captured when fully grown. They are the smartest, but also the most difficult of all to birds to work with Training them was not for the timid, as they could be truly dangerous. What was required was to slowly build up trust.

Birds see more than humans. They can perceive a wider range of colors and the tiniest movement many hundreds of feet below, including air currents rising, essential to be able to soar on updrafts. They themselves can communicate among each other by the tiniest body and feather changes. By careful observation Pir learned to attune to his bird's mood. By the way it held its head and the set of its feathers he could know when it was calm, frightened, or angry. He was gradually learning not just to see as the birds saw, but to feel what they felt. It required patience, and remarkable sensitivity. In the end, he told us that he learned how to enter the birds' consciousness.

Actually, they were both being trained. He was learning skills that would in time be required of a spiritual teacher; the birds were learning something of being human. In this way does the whole of creation evolve, slowly learning more complex abilities and perfecting new qualities in its gradual ascent.

At times the bird's mood would reflect his own. If he moved too quickly, or came too close too soon, the bird might panic or even attack. Ever so slowly fear could be turned into trust. Each bird offered a new challenge. With their superior intelligence, the Eagles would test him. Sometimes it would come down to a contest of wills. Would he manage to put on its hood when he wanted, or when the eagle was ready?

He did not teach his birds to hunt, nor had they been raised by mothers from whom they could learn to kill their own food. They inherit the instinct, but needed training to perfect it. Killing was not Vilayat's way; it was just as well, as many people walked their dogs in the Bois de Boulogne where he took his birds to fly and small dogs would have been at risk from an eagle. It also made it more likely that his birds would return when they flew in the mountains, since they could not feed themselves in the wild. On one occasion one of his eagles flew off for three days, and he believed that he had lost it. In the end it returned when driven by hunger. Once it was attacked by another pair of eagles, which was a frightening but spectacular sight. In the end the bird had to fly back to him for protection. Until he managed to have some of his own, his birds would be his children.

Once he had trained one, then he could share its joy each time he took the leather jesses off its feet and the eagle could fly at last. As the bird soared higher and higher it was almost as if he was flying with it up there, sharing its new found freedom and exultation.

It would be some years before he could indulge himself this way again. After his discharge from the Royal Navy, Vilayat returned to school at Oxford hoping to complete his studies, but poverty forced him to seek work. What he earned at an armed services commissariat was so meager that there was barely enough to provide food for the family. Finally in 1947, he landed a better job with the newly formed Government of Pakistan. Soon his main task would be to help set up conferences. Increasingly the work took him to

Paris, enabling him to move back to Fazal Manzil and soon Claire and his mother could move back as well. It had been taken over by the Germans during the war, and afterwards was used to house wounded soldiers. The house had been allowed to deteriorate over the years. The heating system was no longer functioning, which meant using coal stoves in each room and hauling coal up two or three flights of stairs from the basement. Funds were so short that they were forced to rent out space to a doctor whose patients would walk in and out through the house at all hours, making life there difficult indeed.

Even at war's end there had been no news of Noor. It took many months of anxious waiting until they finally learned what had happened. The horror of it remained with Vilayat all his life. As he remembered:

> I was at the trial afterward. There I heard the details of the capture: how the Nazi who arrested Noor had received a telephone call from a Frenchwoman who said she had the address of my sister and wanted to sell it for 100,000 francs. The Nazi met her on a bench near the Parc Monceau in Paris, and the transaction was made. The consequence of this betrayal was that the brother of this very woman, as well as hundreds of other people, were arrested and tortured. I saw that woman at the trial. She was acquitted by the judge because the lawyer said, "We've suffered enough through the Nazis, and now it is a Nazi who is the only witness here against our French people."
>
> I must say that when I think of the woman who gave away my sister, Noor, and the tragic consequences it had, it's difficult for me not to feel resentment. Similarly, I have tried to forgive the Nazi who beat and kicked her to death, then left her to lie bleeding throughout the night. What has made it somewhat easier for me to understand how one human being could do that to another is knowing that the Nazis used psychopaths as jailers. Thus, when I consider the fact that the man might have been brought up by a stepfather who was a drunk, or who beat him or kicked him out of the house, my resentment is not as easy to sustain. I have a more difficult time reconciling with the woman who betrayed Noor's life for money. So you can imagine how shattered I was, how shattered my mother and sister were.

As if that were not enough, Vilayat's fiancée, with whom he was deeply in love, was killed while riding behind him on his motorcycle. He was taking her to meet his mother and the kickstand came loose and caught in the wheel. They were both thrown off and she never regained consciousness. He was devastated and as a result sunk into a depression that took a long time to heal. Vilayat told what happened then:

> Not too long afterwards I came to see my uncle Maheboob Khan, the younger brother of my father, who had stayed in Holland and had suffered very much. It had been planned for me to take over the leadership of the Sufi Movement. And he had tears in his eyes and he said, "Vilayat, I hope you don't think that I am taking your position away from you. I am just waiting for you to be ready. But now I'd like you to be my first assistant and then I will pass it on to you more and more." And I said, "Well, you know I can't stand facing people now." I was so shattered by it all that I said, "I won't be able to do it. It will take me some time to recover."
>
> I wished that my other uncle (Ali Khan), who was really a cousin of my father, would have given me the support that my first uncle gave me and the kind of support that I'm giving my son. But it was the other way around. My second uncle felt that he needed to give me training to be the successor of Pir-O-Murshid Inayat Khan. He exposed me to a most drastic test, which was to give up my claim to be my father's successor. It was probably his way of destroying my ego to the utmost. And I would have respected it if that was the only question. The reason why I couldn't do it was because I would be foregoing my father's wish, but I couldn't go counter to my father's wish and make its application subject to my uncle's decision. I don't want to be judgmental. Looking back, I was nominated by my father and I was intent on honoring my father's wish; it wasn't mine to give away. But it is possible I needed more maturity. I had to go through life. So I see sense there. One could be judgmental and say well it was usurping a position. But now, I'm a little more mild in my judgment about that whole situation. As Goethe said, "That which you inherit from your ancestors, if you would claim it, you must earn it."

In 1949 he was to receive another severe blow, when his mother died in his arms in great pain from an intestinal blockage. He believed that this tragedy could have been averted if only he had gotten there earlier. To make matters worse, through a mistake for which he also blamed himself, they could never know where her grave was.

The loss of his father followed by the virtual loss of their mother, then the final loss of sister and fiancée and then his mother's death as well, were overwhelming. Although he could never have prevented any of these tragedies, he still blamed himself. Most likely he was never able to fully heal the wounds from the losses of everyone most dear to him.

Who would suspect that this being, who gave so much joy to so many, carried such burdens all of his life, most of which he kept to himself? The Sufis say that the heart must be broken again and again to be able to be fit as a container for Divine Love. However, now there was no one left with whom he could unburden himself, nor did he have the therapeutic tools that are available today.

In the end his salvation was music which he discovered was the only way that he could lift himself out of his despair, and which he hoped could also heal other as well as well, but music could only do so much. When he talked of Noor's death we could all share some of his pain. This is one of the many times he talked of it:

> To understand the extreme importance that music plays in my life, I should tell you that I was once cured from the very depths of despair by playing the High Mass of Bach every day for about two or three months. Maybe it is necessary to have experienced the depths of despair in order to be able to communicate joy to people. I can bear testimony to the fact that music can have the most incredible therapeutic value that one could ever imagine. I assume that it would work on other people as dramatically, but I can't be sure, because music means more to some people than others.

His work involved much travel. He became an assistant to the Pakistani finance minister, Ghulam Mohammed. This was unusual for a thirty-three year old with no prior work experience. Ghulam was a Sufi and he remembered his murshid telling him about a great master in Europe; that teacher was none other than Hazrat Inayat Khan. Ghulam was not an easy man to work for. Vilayat explained that, "He had a way of saying, 'No' in a way that brooked no discussion." He once explained how he learned this. His first teacher who had begun training him in the dhikr had died before Ghulam had time to go beyond the first part, which starts with the *La* — "no." The result was that he was elevated to the position of finance minister, who needs to be able to say "no." When Liaquat Ali Khan, the Prime Minister, came to England for the Sterling Conference, Vilayat became his personal assistant. He was justifiably proud of such important responsibilities. For the first time in his adult life, money was no longer a problem.

It was during this period that he met his future wife, the lovely Mary Walls. He found her a job at the same office. She adored him, and her cheerful personality also helped lift him out of his depression. According to her, she almost died of tuberculosis and was convinced that he healed her. She said that he healed several others as well. Eventually they decided to marry; she was Catholic, so they were married by a priest. However, she was not able to have children, and explained that she had never wanted them. Soon they would be a move to France and live at Fazal Manzil with his sister Claire and their mother. She and Claire became quite close. Claire had always relied on Vilayat for support, but he was often away, and Mary could run the household and provide much needed strength and cheer.

Mary was also an intrepid traveler like Vilayat and was not afraid of hard conditions or danger. Starting in the early 50s they were to go to India almost every year. She shared his love of the East, although she did not go with him on his trips into the high mountains. In 1955 he was able to get a VW Bus, in which they drove overland three times. On one of these trips Vilayat had a close call. Since money was short, they took along someone they did not know to share expenses. He was a communist spy and was caught taking forbidden photographs. Just before they were interrogated by the police, he dropped his tiny Minox camera into Vilayat's boot; by luck it was not found.

Throughout his life, Vilayat's concern for the exploited drove him to fight injustice. However, his hatred of injustice clearly outweighed his prudence. Between 1951 and 1953 he wrote articles for *Dawn*, the outspoken Pakistani newspaper, which revealed how the French were using torture against the Algerian rebels, as well as putting pressure on the king of Morocco. The resulting dossier no doubt contributed to future problems with the French authorities. Not surprisingly, he became unwelcome in Algeria. He was always prone to taking risks.

Once to avoid being stopped he sneaked across the border by riding a camel through the Moroccan dessert. When Algeria finally gained independence despite the power of the French Army, it was largely as a result of media coverage of the war. He once explained that he thought this work helped him to lift some of the burden of his guilt for not having stopped Noor from joining the military. Perhaps this would be another reason why he would do so much to help the poor and downtrodden later one.

The pull of his destiny would also exert itself more and more strongly. In *The Hero with a Thousand Faces*, Joseph Campbell wrote that if the hero doesn't heed the call to action, "the flowering world becomes a wasteland of dry stones." His war experiences had both matured him and strengthened his dedication. He wrote, "I decided to work with all my heart for what I was born for: The Message of Hazrat Inayat Khan." He began to devote himself to what would become a lifelong study of his father's work and of the different religions. In the process he would go deeply into Islam and even learn parts of the Koran by heart. He was also increasingly drawn to meditation and remembered his first rather unexpected experience of samadhi years earlier in the garden of Fazal Manzil. He said "I needed to figure out how I got there."

At the time while he was studying philosophy and psychology at Oxford, he was bothered by the contradictions with what he was studying and his fathers ideas. Perhaps that was why he failed an examination. That summer he took his books with him to the French Alps. There in Chamonix, surrounded by the glorious mountains he discovered that he was able to absorb what he needed and passed the examination with ease. He had found his perfect place and would keep on returning every summer to hike and meditate. It was during one of these excursions that he discovered what would become the cave he had always longed for.

Vilayat's experience of Christianity had started early, when Fazl Mai would sometimes taken the children to church with her.

Then there had been his Catholic tutor whose strong faith had so deeply impressed him. Years later he was drawn to do retreats both on the Mount of Olives in Jerusalem in a cave where he believed Jesus spent time, and also at the monastery in Montserrat in Spain. High above there were also caves which had long been used by monks for their own retreats.

Montserrat was where Tomás Luis de Victoria had lived and written his music. Some of this was to remain a major inspiration all of Vilayat's life. He related how deeply moved he had been by the vespers service there, and the deep impressions left by the sight of people being transformed as they received communion.

In the future he would be able to share these and other moving experiences with us. One example that he could recall was how as he listened to Bach being played on the organ in a small church, his spirit soared upwards through levels of ever more refined light. His memories of these experiences were so vivid that we felt as if we were there with him sharing in his joy. His was a rare gift indeed. Here is what he wrote of another such memorable time:

There was a young man who conducted the B Minor Mass

in the church of Naarden in Holland, that I attended. He lived it, and inspired everyone. During all of it I was able to see the conductor's face. He was going through the whole experience that Bach himself had gone through, the experience of the Passion of Christ and the Resurrection."

In 1965 Vilayat organized his first interfaith congress, where he got the opportunity to meet with leaders of other traditions. He learned much in the process, but the primary purpose was to foster greater understanding between the different faiths.

One result was that his growing interest in religion led him to do an extensive study of angels in the different traditions. At one point he actually contemplated getting a PhD on the subject himself. Many years later, in his late seventies, on seeing a beautiful book of angels, he said, "This is the book I always dreamed of writing." However, by that time he had learned to contact angelic beings directly and was thus able to tell us about them. I wondered how many mystics over the ages have ever been able to do as much.

Chapter 4
RISHIS AND HERMITS

Do not found your hopes on what is transient, do not rejoice in having attained the inestimable, for you will again narrow it down to a possession. Do not pursue joy but let it pursue you. Your very ideal proves to be a product of your own mind. Know that it is the supreme test, forcing you to become your real self, because you are not allowed to walk with crutches any more, or to stand on illusion.

Dare you be in the world and not of the world? Dare you have possessions without being possessed?

— PIR VILAYAT INAYAT KHAN

In 1949 Vilayat was at last able to start his search for great masters. On the way to India he spent time in Iran. There he saw dervishes in ragged clothing who would greet one another like royalty. He felt the emotion of powerful dhikrs for the first time. He recounted:

> I remember in Iran there was a picture of a dervish in the window of the shop selling all kinds of things. One look at that face and I said, "Oh, I have never seen a man like this. Incredible! So much joy, so much suffering!" I went inside and asked, "Can you tell me who that is?" He looked at me, burst into tears and said, "He was a great dervish, my father. I just buried him three days ago." I missed him by three days!

> I attended a meeting at a place called Haftan-dervish, meaning seventy dervishes, in Shiraz. There is a source of water coming out of the rocks; it's an enchanting place. You sit there on Thursday evening when they have dhikr; you see people who are so illuminated, their faces are transfigured by what they are saying. They are quoting Sufi poets and conversing using expressions from

Sufi poetry. One says, "I wish I could see God," and the other says, "Oh remove this veil standing between thou and me." And another says, "The face of God is the form of all beings." "Yes, but they cover the reality of God." "How can I do away with my face?"

These were his first tantalizing tastes of the Sufis which up till then he had only read about. Clearly he had to continue his search but he remembered how enthralled he was by the exquisite Persian architecture, one of man's finest expressions of the sublime, which he also felt in the singing of Abdulwahab Shahidi, filled as it was with longing for the Beloved. Year later he would share some of his memories with us when he played that music. This gave me the inspiration to find more of this great music for him and then find a way make it available for all the rest of us. This would become my vocation.

What he was embarking on was the archetypical hero's journey. Joseph Campbell described it in *The Hero with a Thousand Faces* as follows:

A hero ventures forth from the world of common day into a region of supernatural wonder: fabulous forces are there encountered and a decisive victory is won: the hero comes back from this mysterious adventure with the power to bestow boons on his fellow man.

On the journey there is always a great longing for a mysterious quest that must be undertaken. It is a metaphor for the deep inner journey of transformation. Before the quest can be started, a great obstacle has to be overcome. Next the seeker is given advice from a wise man. Then the hero faces tests, which often take the form of a life-or-death crisis followed by a disappointment. Finally overcoming all the obstacles, he reaches his destination and obtains the treasure, which is often described as an elixir. The hero has been resurrected, purified, and has earned the right to be accepted back into the ordinary world and to share the elixir won in his journey.

Vilayat's father had said that the greatest rishis were at a secret place "where the two rivers meet." These were the two holy rivers, the Jumna and Ganga or Ganges, which seemed to originate in different places. He met a sannyasin who gave him an important clue to the mystery; the secret place was to be found under the glaciers! It would require going far above Kedernath, which was itself at an elevation of almost 12,000 feet. He could never resist challenges, especially when they involved high climbing. Here is one of the many times he recounted it:

I was still quite young when I had my first encounter with a rishi sitting in a cave. I had come a long way. I had walked three days in the snow, and I had caught pneumonia. I was also rather scared, because there were tracks in the snow that I thought might be the tracks of a bear, and bears are quite dangerous in the Himalayas. I followed the tracks anyway, in the hope that they were the footsteps of a human being, and they turned out to be the tracks of a rishi. The first thing he said to me was, "Why have you come so far to see what you should be?" I was still rather inexperienced, so I just said, "It is wonderful to see this." Today, I suppose I would have said, "To become what I should be I have to see myself in you".

By this time he was soaked, shivering, and running a fever which forced him to go back down. Still he had passed a test and the rishi told him to come back when he was well. First, however, he had another test to pass. This time he was stopped by the police. The area was restricted and foreigners were not permitted. He was detained, but by jumping out of a rear window he escaped and managed to go up again.

Now the rishi was willing to talk, although his manner was distant and severe. However, he gave him some practices to do. Vilayat found another cave and remained to try what he had been told.

This was just the first of many trips he made in search of great masters. One wonders if perhaps he may have subconsciously been hoping to find a being like the father he had lost in these searches. Here is his account of another meeting:

> When I was very young, I visited a rishi in Badrinof, which is above Rishikesh, somewhere on the way up to the source of the Ganges. It was a holy place attracting many pilgrims. There was a hot water spring, and this rishi was sitting next to it. I wasn't familiar with the customs. I couldn't see myself bowing my head down to a rishi, and the whole thing looked a little bit strange to me at that time. Now, of course, it is very familiar. He pointed to me: "You come." I came, and I greeted him and sat next to him. He started speaking, and he taught me more and more things. Then he asked me to come back every day, and I sat there for hours with him. I really learned a lot from him.
>
> In the meantime, people were coming and bowing their heads at his feet. He said to me, "I shall be moving to Kedernath." Kedernath is on the way up to the Jumna, which is another river higher up. So I said, "Well, why?" He said, "Well, there's a post." That was the word he used, post, "for each of us to sit on." He sat there at a post, and there was a time when he was promoted to another post. So it's just like a government in which there are certain positions. There are offices, and you may be promoted to another position. Then somebody else has to fill in that post. I said to him, "How will you know?" He said, "I'll know." That was all.

This was his first tantalizing contact with a member of the Spiritual Hierarchy. Overcome by curiosity, Vilayat tried to go further himself, even though the rishi had told him it was time for him to go

down. Soon someone else stopped him and told him not to go on. At
these altitudes the need for rests become more frequent. No matter
how deep one breathes the lungs cry out for sustenance that is not
there. Each step becomes another challenge. He pushed himself to go
on until he was met again and told firmly "You are not permitted to go
here." *Who were these beings at these remote locations and how did they
know?* Vilayat wondered.

Inspired by the example of the sannyasins and what he had learned
from them, he began to do more retreats in mountain caves. Here is
one story he told about that period in his life in the early 1950s:

> I lived as a sannyasin in a cave at the source of the Ganges in
> Gangotri. That was a very extraordinary experience. It was quite
> wonderful to be out of the world like that. I would be walking with
> my beggar's bowl and I tried to pay for my food in the shops where
> they sold rice and dahl, but they would never let me. Once when
> I was sitting in my cave it was very cold. I had collected wood to
> make a fire, but I couldn't see how I could keep on putting logs on
> the fire if I was in samadhi. When my front was warm my back
> would be cold, so it made no sense anyway. So I left the cave and
> stepped across the water where it was not very deep and sat on an
> island to meditate. What I wanted to do was to remember exactly
> how I got into samadhi so I could teach it. At a certain moment
> I lost consciousness and all I remember was that when the sun
> rose and I was a little thawed out, I found myself surrounded by
> a group of sannyasins who thought that I had attained samadhi.
> Actually, all that had happened was that I had frozen to death.

Well perhaps, however, if he died before death and resurrected no
frost damage was apparent. Most likely he did not want to boast and
clearly he had learned how to get back into samadhi by that time. But
there are levels of samadhi and he of course always hoped to go further.
Sometimes there is a trace of envy in his descriptions:

> I can give you an example of another rishi I saw once above
> Kedernath in mountains about fifteen thousand feet high. It was
> very cold; the mountains were covered in snow. And the dawn was
> lifting upon the mountain peaks gloriously. And there he sat naked
> in the snow. His body was as white as snow and even the retina of

his eyes had become a little bit albino. And he sat there like a rock without stirring, and his whole being reflected the glistening of the snow and the diaphanous light of the sunrise. And he seemed part of the mountain vastness. He was not a person. He was like the substrata out of which life is made. There was no strife in him, no heartaches, no soul-searchings, no sadness, no joy, no anger. Not even sovereignty. He was just neutral. He was the epitome of samadhi.

I have met rishis way up, above 14,000, who were living there permanently; there is no food up there, nobody ever comes up there, so they are living without food. I have seen them rub rocks together, and make a powder of it in the water, so they get the minerals that are needed for survival. But there is no source of carbohydrates or fats or protein of any kind. How do they manage? I put it down to photosynthesis.

One of the highest beings that Vilayat met was Baba Sita Ramdas Omkarnath, who he called "The greatest rishi in India." Pir said that he was barely in his body and all his bones and veins were showing. All he ate was an apple every few days. Their meeting was quite extraordinary.

Here is one account Pir wrote:

> I went to see him. ... I don't know what happened to us, but we were just totally moved to tears. He couldn't stop hugging me. ... His body was cold as ice, and I was giving him all my energy. We were all in tears, absolutely overwhelmed by what was happening. He said, "We are the same being," words that are beyond the usual way of speaking, and that was exactly how it felt. I have met many gurus in my life, and I have never experienced anything like that closeness. That was unique.

In the start of his search the great souls in the Himalayas attracted him the most. In time however, he would search out hermits in other places. It was on Mount Athos which the Greeks call the Holy Mountain that he had his first encounter with Christian Hesychasts living in huts or under large rocks that they had made habitable high above the sea.

When he talked about it, I sensed that he sounded a bit envious. He wrote:

> I have had a great privilege of coming across some very wonderful hermits in Mount Athos in Greece. Living inside a hut is a monk who has become a hermit. No matter what time of day you come, he will be praying. To talk with the monks you would have to speak Russian, Bulgarian or Greek, although most of them will not speak. These were truly holy men; what that means is their whole being becomes golden. It's the most valuable thing in the world. Just imagine the feeling amongst the early Christians in the catacombs with their dedication to the living Christ.

Pir suggested I go to Mount Athos on my way to India. Perhaps he knew of special reasons which I would soon come to realize. Only twelve permits are issued each day to visitors who were not Orthodox. When I arrived at the building in Thessalonika I found that at least twenty people were all ready waiting. When the gate opened they all rushed ahead. Realizing that I did not have a chance I took my time. Someone directed me to the proper office where I was given my permit at which point all the others breathlessly arrived. They had all been misdirected!

I stayed at the monastery of Saint Panteleimon. He is revered as one of the great Orthodox healing saints. I prayed to him for healing as I had been suffering from an illness that left me unable to digest food. My prayer was answered and the problem disappeared; it had been a test which I passed when I had taken the risk of leaving all my medication in Thessalonika before I traveled to the Holy Mountain.

To my surprise I discovered that the monks in this holy place were still fighting old battles. Byzantium had been fatally weakened by the Crusaders during the fourth crusade when crusaders had captured Mount Athos and sacked the monasteries. The monks still held this against Rome which had ignored the Byzantine Emperor's pleas for help and yet they chose to forget that their own church had rejected overtures to reunite with the Catholics based on differing ideas about the nature of Christ and rituals. For the monks in this stronghold of orthodoxy events what happened in the 15th Century were more real than the recent world wars.

Despite that, based on my healing and another powerful experience it was clear that there was much holiness here. That happened when I visited a small chapel inside the monastery of Stavronikita looking like a Medieval fortress perched on a cliff high above the Aegean.

There an unseen force pushed me to my knees where I remained in an altered state for I know not how long, until later in the day I felt a monk's hand on my shoulder telling me that it was time to leave.

While Pir Vilayat would continue to search for great beings from various traditions, increasingly his inspiration would come from the great Sufis of the past as he became better able to contact them. Initially it would be with Al Hallaj but also in time Ibn Arabi and Shahabuddin Suhrawardi. He would explain to us that it is possible to contact any being if you can reach high enough. He also told us that it had taken him a number of years before he was able to reach his father.

On Retreat

Trekking

Chapter 5
A Dervish in the Making

*Involve yourself in the Divine Plan and know how to resign yourself to
the Divine Will, so that you become as an inert body in the hands of the One
who washes it; and at the same time your will becomes as strong as that of a
lion. Only then does one become truly free.*

*The dervish severs every bond systematically except the Friend, the
most precious treasure on earth. He takes upon himself the sufferings of men,
transmuting them with joy. When he has been transformed, the dervish
walks throughout the streets with the majesty of a king.*

— Pir Vilayat Inayat Khan

Pir Vilayat rarely spoke of his Sufi training. It had actually started
with his uncle Sheikh Maheboob Khan, who first taught him the dhikr.
He wrote that Aziz Miyan of Bareilly next continued this training. He
then went on to Hyderabad where he met Pir Jili Kaleemi who headed
another branch of the Chishtiyya. His son Pir Rashid said this meeting
took place in January of 1950. His father's full name was Sayyid Fakhr-
ud-din ul-Hasan Jeeli Kaleemi and his father, Rashid's grandfather, had
been a teacher of Abu Hashim Madani, Inayat Khan's teacher. Thus the
two lineages were interconnected.

Rashid's father told him that he remembered that Vilayat was
dressed in the local style, a kurta (long shirt) and loose cotton pants.
One day when he was in a mystical state he had a vision of Hazrat
Inayat Khan, who told him to tell Vilayat, "Last night I received a
message from your father, that I must train you for your position as a
Pir-o-Murshid. I must give you *bayat* and the classical training." Vilayat
answered, "Oh I can't do that, because my murshid is my father." Pir
Jeeli Kaleemi replied, "Oh yes, I will always respect that. I am only a
mentor for you." Vilayat agreed and he received an initiation from him.

Rashid remembered that Vilayat would come every morning for several months to be instructed for an hour or two. As his father spoke no English, he translated for them before he went to work. In time Rashid was to succeed him and became a Murshid in his own right. His father had suggested that Vilayat do a retreat in the small dargah of Baba Pahari, on a rocky hill in Hyderabad. Here is the way Pir remembered it:

> He said "When you're doing the dhikr, you should just get into your father's consciousness." And that's what establishes a link, you see. Don't do the dhikr as though you're doing it yourself.... That's how I was doing the dhikr, 22,000 times a day.
>
> Getting into my father's consciousness, I got into the consciousness of Abu Hashim Madani and getting into his consciousness, I got into the consciousness of his father and of course there I was sitting at the tomb of his father.
>
> And so Pir Kaleemi came in to call me for prayer. He said, "Vilayat" and I thought, the name is familiar but I couldn't even recognize myself... And then he looked at me and he said, "You've seen my father." So he saw the expression of his father; that shows that it really works.

Hazrat Inayat Khan grew up within the traditional Sufi culture of Baroda, where deep respect for one's elders, and especially the murshid, was universal. When he first came to the West, Inayat was appalled by the lack of *adab* of his mureeds. Adab translates as the knowledge of proper conduct, dedication to service, and of course, respect for the teacher. This was mostly lacking in the West and Inayat was at a loss as how to go about teaching it. In the East all of this is imbibed by children within the family and taught by the mureeds to each other, as well as by the teacher's example. It was hard for him to do this as most mureeds only saw him during his talks. In Sufi groups the students could ask questions and get guidance from their Murshid every week. Here he had to learn Western ways and there were so few cultural parallels for him to fall back on. Also many esoteric practices could not be shared in talks to large groups. In the end, so much of his rich heritage was diluted, and much was inevitably lost in this first attempt to transfer it to the West.

Traditional Sufi training is given to the mureeds by the murshid during the weekly *sohbets*, where the student could sit at the feet of the teacher. Vilayat's training could not be this way as he had received a Western upbringing and his father had died when he was young. There was not even any male figure for him to emulate. As his time was limited, the purpose now was to prepare him for his coming role as a murshid and Pir of an order.

Until he traveled to the East what Vilayat knew about Sufism was of necessity limited to written sources as there were no Sufi teachers in Europe at that time. Of these sources, the most important were his father's lectures and esoteric papers. In his travels he made it a point to collect as many books as he could, but these were mostly in Persian or Urdu which he could not read. However, these were to prove useful in time for his son Zia who learned both languages.

Vilayat's enthusiasm for India helped him overcome the difficulties he faced there. Lofty spirituality and debased rituals, joy and suffering, as well as kindness and cruelty were often in close proximity. Mary spoke of his fury at the corruption and cruelty he encountered on their early trips there. All this was of course part of his inheritance, an inheritance which was also a source of great pride for him.

Tipu Sultan, one of the greatest Indian heroes, was one of his ancestors. He was a great military commander, as well as a poet and scholar, and was also an implacable enemy of the British He was nicknamed the 'Tiger of Mysore.' This was in the late 1700s when the East India Company was in the process of taking over the subcontinent. Even Napoleon sought an alliance with Tipu, who came quite close to defeating the British. They held him in such high esteem that he was given a military funeral with full honors. Vilayat had his personal seal with a tiger on it, of which he was quite proud.

Some of his fondest memories were of Ajmer, where tombs (*dargahs*) of the most famous of the Chishti saints are located. Vilayat did several long retreats there. In the 1950s he was there for the death anniversary or *urs* celebrations which attracted many thousands of Sufis from all of Asia.

He loved to recount some of his experiences there:

> On a Pilgrimage to Ajmer about a hundred thousand people had converged on the tomb of Moinuddin Chishti. Some of them from Mongolia, Libya, and China. At night, listening to the musicians extemporize on the verses of the Sufi poets, some of the dervishes who were carried beyond themselves began to gyrate; this is the dervish dance. Their souls soaring higher and higher. When the murshid leaves, the dervishes continue their dhikr, conversing in song and gesture, communicating their ecstasy to each other, their souls soaring higher and higher. The whole crowd seemed to come under some magic spell. One of the songs was *Allah Hu*. They went on and on and the whole company was in a state of rapt intoxication, a breath of God was blowing upon their souls.

That was when he had his first experience of a *madzub*, a powerful, God-intoxicated being. The night before, Vilayat had been told, a dervish had come looking for him. He waited up for him and finally went to sleep. Late that night he was awakening by pounding on his door, but at the sound of his raucous voice Vilayat had huddled deeper in his sleeping bag. The next night he slept in the dargah. He tells how he sat on the cold stones, tightly surrounded by hundreds of unwashed bodies, many dressed in rags:

> Towards four o'clock in the morning, I was meditating on the marble floor of the dargah, surrounded by a compact row of pilgrims, and by others singing hymns to the saints, and the glory of God. The voice of the madzub drew closer, the harmonics so deep that they seized the soul in awe. He did not beckon, he commanded. Standing erect though resting on a cane, with the detachment of one who has known the solitude of the caves, he scanned all the astonished crowd which had assembled, and said, "You there!"

In that moment something happened, Vilayat said he was never quite the same. Exactly what had happened he did not say. However the experience was so powerful and the atmosphere so magical that he would return there on several other occasions. Here is his account of what it was like on another occasion:

> I was sitting in Ajmer at the tomb of Khwaja Moinuddin Chishti, repeating the dhikr. And there was a musician sitting under some columns there on the left. There were very few people about. And he was singing with his whole heart and playing the tambura. I was moved to ecstasy by his being. It was so mystically powerful, what was coming through him, that I didn't even dare look at him. And somehow at one time I felt I just couldn't resist it and I just turned and looked at him. He stood up and he came towards me and he said, "I have a message from your father." And at that moment he looked exactly like Murshid. And he said, "When you do the dhikr, when you say illa 'llah hu, turn within instead of turning upwards. You're turning upwards, and that's a stage in the dhikr, but now you have reached a stage when you should do the internal dhikr. Just turn within." It's said this is the dhikr of the broken heart because the heart of God is wounded. You can imagine how that affected me, and I started doing it.

The next time he came to Ajmir it was to do a forty day retreat. The sheikh gave him *wazifas* (Arabic mantras) to repeat:

> I was feeling so high, experiencing all the divine qualities, when a murshid came to me and said, "The time has now come for you to meditate solely upon the divine presence." I said, "Here I am meditating all the day on the divine attributes, it's so rich and wonderful. Do you mean the Divine Being beyond qualities?" "Yes," he said, "No qualities, just the divine presence." "Well I couldn't do that. My mind would have no patterns to weave upon." "You'll do it, you'll do it," he said. "How can I do it?" "By repeating the dhikr." "How can just repeating the dhikr do that?" "You'll see, you'll see, but only on the condition that you are prepared to be shattered in your sense of the self, otherwise you can't do it." "Yes," I said, "That's exactly what I'd like to do." So I proceeded on a new retreat solely practicing the dhikr.

Pir often contrasted the experience of the dervish with that of the rishi. Whereas the rishi aspires to reach beyond himself, into the Divine Consciousness, the dervish allows himself to be shattered by the Divine Awareness: "One is so shattered there is no vestige of the personal identity left."

Probably he was describing his own experiences such as the time his guide called his name, and he wondered just who was Vilayat. There was another time in a cave on the Mount of Olives. He had to leave each night and as he walked through the streets of Jerusalem he said he felt like a street light shining out all around him:

> You may be enthused by the glory or his love but not the Beloved himself. You must really touch upon the Being of God. Only then are you drowned in that ocean of love. But then you go through agonies and ecstasies and you will be tested in your love. You will be abandoned and betrayed by the very being you love. If you persevere in your love even though there is no reciprocation gradually there will be signs of His Presence like a little light which in time will become like a thousand suns. And then the Divine Presence will dawn and overwhelm you beyond your very horizon. Maybe the next time you will be strengthened a little more, until you are able to maintain the Divine Consciousness continuously.

These were all transformative experiences which involved what he called a "dramatic shift in perspective." It was like the *vajra*, the diamond thunderbolt of the Tibetans, that can strike unexpectedly. He said:

> It's an extraordinary experience when you discover that the frontier between you and others has been removed and there is no separation anymore. There is no subject and object, that is the moment of ecstasy. It was all a mistake to think that the forms and qualities of the world were just a veil. He is in all things, just as I am in all things and in all beings; I am the butterflies and the mountains and the sunrise and the sunset. I am the sinner and the saint, I am the servant and the master and I am love.

Chapter 6
PILGRIMAGES AND RETREAT

*If I were asked what the journey really is, and what its object, I would
answer that the purpose of the whole of creation was for this journey, and
that if it were not for this purpose there would be no creation at all.*
— HAZRAT INAYAT KHAN

*The reason why we are here is to sound the uncharted depths of the
Universe and realize that is our self. Like the Buddha said, there is a place
you reach without going anywhere. We think we are an individual, but
what we actually are is the totality.*
— PIR VILAYAT INAYAT KHAN

His early days in India filled as they were with encounters with
dervishes and rishis, were some of the happiest times in Vilayat's
life up until that point. His memories were so vivid he seemed to be
living them again in the telling. He had a special gift of sharing their
flavor in a way that carried us along with him, so that we shared in his
enthusiasm. Naturally in the process he kindled our hopes of meeting
great beings as well. He made it a practice to go to his father's tomb
each year on February 5th the anniversary of his death (*urs*). The result
was that he started taking small groups with him to India.

One year without telling him, the local mullah wrapped his head
in a special turban reserved for especially holy beings. On leaving
Nizamuddin Aulia's dargah, hordes of people pushed and shoved
trying to touch him hoping for a healing or protection. The situation
was dangerous as mob hysteria began to take over. He was saved by
quick thinking, and jumped into a motor rickshaw and managed to
escape the most determined pursuers. Incidents like this made India
an ongoing challenge for him, yet he would always return year after

year in time for the anniversary of his father's death.

These holy places attracted pilgrims and dervishes from all over Asia. It was common to see people sobbing on their knees or while kissing the cloth covering the tomb of Moinuddin Chisti, while others seemed lost in ecstasy. Such scenes of devotion are unlike anything any of us had ever seen before.

Another year a strange dervish dressed in a ragged black robe with long white hair streaming down his back led the procession. He was silent, masterful, but remote, a striking example of the divine majesty When he chanted "Haqq " (Truth) it filled the room like a great hammer blow. We would have loved to talk with him, but none of us dared try.

Over the years we were to meet many other powerful beings. Sheikh Muzzafer of the Helveti-Jerrahi Order along with his Turkish mureeds, came to New York where he led his dervishes doing dhikr in the Cathedral of Saint John. There an audience of several thousand who joined the chanting. The extraordinary energy generated and that massive sound echoing though the vast space of the huge cathedral ranked high in the list of my most unforgettable memories.

Pir had a deep love for Ajmir, the holy city in the Rajasthan dessert. On one trip with large group, we met a Pir of the Sabri Order. His deep voice and great sheepskin coat added to his own massive presence. He had come down from the Baltistan region of Northern Pakistan near Hunza. He and Pir Vilayat hit it off immediately and seemed like old friends. They spoke of their work as being like that of two old elephants, bringing in the untrained ones (us) to be tamed. The Sabri Sheikh had the feel of a mountain man about him. His home was near K2, the second tallest mountain in the world, which clearly put Pir Vilayat's mind unto high places.

Several times Pir Vilayat brought groups to his favorite spot on a small mountain above Ajmer where the caves of Moinuddin Chishti and his disciple Bakhtiyar Kaki were located. Vilayat had done two forty day retreats there during which he said he had felt guided by their souls. As the rays of the rising sun reached us, Pir's face seemed to become luminous.

He said, "The sun is your ancestor. To look at the sun you must have eyes like the sun. You must discover your solar heritage, and then reach beyond the sun into the sun of the sun of the solar system, which is the sun of the galaxy, and then beyond until you get into what Sufis call *Nour al Anwar*, the all pervading Light of Lights." The pull out into the galaxy had always been strong for him, but his final advice before his death was "You must think galactically" and "Once we have broken bread together we will always be connected. We will meet again in the stars."

Over the years Pir acquired a number of caves but none could compare with his favorite high above Chamonix in the French Alps. Once he spoke of it this way: "I suppose you can feel the whole tradition of the rishis of India is very strong in me. I have this cave, which has a view over Mont Blanc and the whole Mer de Glace, the most beautiful scenery in the world." From there he could look out on what he described as "so many glistening cathedral spires, rising above vast glaciers below." It was here in the clean cold air that the hermit in him could feel truly at home.

During the 1960s he had been giving small summer meditation camps in the Austrian and Swiss Alps. Leading a group retreat above Chamonix did not seem practical as it was so inaccessible. Finally however, a few hardy souls accompanied him and a new tradition was started. When he had first found it, what would become his cave was just a space under two rocks, but he knew that it had great possibilities. There was an opening at the top which could let smoke out and there was water near by. Gradually we improved it. A tiny stream was diverted to supply enough water for his tea and morning cereal. A sleeping platform was added with a rope ladder. There he could tuck himself in up close to the rocks where he always felt most at home.

In the beginning the groups were quite small. Everything had to be carried up over a mile from the cable car. As nothing could be left there, it all had to be laboriously carried down again at the end. Peanut butter, cereal and bread were the main staples. At the start he not only led the camp by himself, but often did much of the cooking as well. He also managed to lead the sessions in three languages. There was one large tent for everything. All of this required strenuous effort and much dedication, but how glorious it was!

He loved to lead us in greeting the rising sun with resounding "Ya Fattahs." One year someone got a donkey for Pir to ride up on. In the high clear air, so close to the clouds, it was easy for him to elevate all of us and on one occasion the enthusiasm was so great that even the donkey was seen to dance.

The word spread, and as more people came, the logistics became impractical. Pir made the decision to relocate to a more accessible site in the French Alps which he called the "The camp of the eagles," but it could never be the same. In no way could the views compare. After several years it moved again to Switzerland, but by then food and tents were needed for as many as three hundred people which meant they had to be accessible by trucks. As Pir wrote, "When the camp couldn't stay in Chamonix any longer, it broke my heart because that cave meant so much to me."

Whenever possible he tried to lead his events in inspiring natural settings, the higher the better. He knew that what helped lift our attunement and help us to experience refined emotions could help cultivate similar qualities in our own souls. With more students and better organization, trips to the Himalayas even became possible. On the second of these trips he brought a group to Nilkanth high above the city of Rishikesh filled with ashrams and sadhus.

Most of us hiked up for several hours, but Pir did it in style: he rode on an elephant. No one had ever tried this before, and there was doubt if it could even be possible. The sight attracted locals from the whole surrounding area. As high as he went, he always wanted to go higher. My challenge was to get all the mics, batteries, recorders and speakers up to ever higher altitudes so we could all hear him.

Pir had long hoped go back to Gangotri to recapture some of the

India he had known in the early days in, but that would be difficult. He told us that it was mostly all gone now.

We had to wait several days until the road could be cleared of snow. Rather than waiting, Pir hiked in so that he could do a short retreat by himself. Even before we arrived a rumor had spread that there were a group of Muslims coming to this most sacred of Hindu holy places. Two of the sadhus were suspicious and followed us to the great cave where that he had used years before. They stood in the back listening to the meditation which he led. Not surprisingly what he did was based on what he had learned years before from the sadhus themselves.

Gangotri is over 10,000 feet in elevation. The air was crisp and energizing. The Ganges flows swiftly as it emerges from the glacier not far above. Here in the high mountains he so loved Pir's hermit side could emerge. No doubt here had the freedom to become more himself. Our days here went by all too quickly.

Pir's cave in Esperero Canyon, outside Tucson Arizona, was nestled in a remote canyon in the Sonoran dessert. To get there required a long hike across a desert dotted with a strange saguaro cactus. These were tall dark green giants, towering twenty or more feet, had great upraised arms jutting out seemingly in attitudes of prayer. Entering the canyon from this vast space one suddenly entered another world, where a crystal clear stream formed limpid pools flanked by ferns, cottonwoods, and willows in every shade of green. At the far end was a narrow waterfall which fell from high above. Merlin, the same student who had crafted his cave in the Alps, had constructed a small one here under a big rock, just large enough for Pir and a small fire.

Pir Vilayat had long wanted to lead a group retreat here, but it would not be practical. We hit upon the idea of filming him there instead. There was a rocky ledge, where he could sit and do dhikr, conveniently next to the waterfall. This was where the stream dropped hundreds of feet from the rocks above all of which made for a most impressive backdrop on film! The plan was to videotape him leading practices. He particularly wanted to do 'Ya Wahabo' sitting beside flowing water. As it turned out, with only the camera to talk to his words sounded forced and artificial, which would never do. Whatever he did, it had to be authentic, always!

This was his second retreat here, his first one had actually been cut short. Then it had been dry for many months, but soon it began to pour. As the waters rose, they reached the point where he was forced to flee, at one point, carrying his precious laptop on his head. However, by then such things had happened so often nothing could surprise him. During his first camp in Florida it snowed! Such events were characteristic of the opposition he faced during his whole life, filled as it was with obstacles which would have daunted most lesser beings. However he persevered and always longed for his next retreat.

Chapter 7
RIDING THE NEW AGE WAVE

We know the real journey occurs in the internal spaces. Where does one go from here? What are our sailing orders?
Fortunate the wayfarer who is briefed by those rare pioneers who chart the uncharted, who brave the depths and spaces of Being, and offer future generations the topologies of internal sites and further spheres.
— PIR VILAYAT INAYAT KHAN

In 1968 Pir Vilayat met Murshid Samuel Lewis. Sam was also a longtime devotee of Inayat Khan. Sam had recently been told in a vision that he was to be "a teacher for the hippies." Sam's student Wali Ali was with them and remembers how Pir talked about the dervishes' dances. When Wali Ali asked where one could find a dervish, Pir Vilayat pointed to Sam and said, "You have one there.

Soon after that Sam began to teach what he called Dervish Dances. He always said Pir Vilayat was the father and he was the mother of the dances. How well Pir recognized his child was another question.

Murshid Sam and Pir Vilayat began to cooperate in 1969 and both began to attract more and more students. Perhaps the two teachers energized one another but the time was also right. Sam's following quickly grew from thirty to sixty students. Pir Vilayat was soon able to open his first center in the US and held his first camp in Colorado as well.

The camp featured the teachings of Inayat Khan, meditations, as well as hatha yoga and Sam's spiritual walks and new dances that he was creating. Most of those who came were Murshid Sam's students, and these included a number of very talented and dedicated followers who would help spread his teachings and dances into the next century. At the start the two teachers cooperated and with the help of Sam's students Pir Vilayat was able to start doing camps and seminars in the US. Hardly anyone knew what a Sufi was, but it didn't matter. Labels were unimportant; it was the experience that counted.

The following year the camp was in Arizona, where parts of the movie *Sunseed* were filmed. It remains the classic film documenting the dawning of the New Age. In one scene the sun was rising behind Pir and something zapped me; at that moment I knew he was to be my teacher.

He began giving seminars in New York and several other cities, attracting mostly young people, many with long hair. Anything was possible in those exciting years when the rising New Age wave would soon begin to attract up to two hundred people to his camps. Soon Pir let his own hair grow; no doubt which came as a shock to his more staid European followers.

The idea of starting a community first came to Vilayat in 1974 at his camp near Woodstock. He said, "I feel that we are part of a tribe. We need a community to shield people from the pressures of the materialistic world." There was an enthusiastic shout: "Yeah!" After a search the decision was made to purchase land in South Carolina. It was rather remote, but the price and weather seemed good. At the last moment, came word of an entire small Shaker Village for sale in northern New York State. It had been the first spiritual community to be founded in 1789 in what would soon become the United States. However, it was not what Pir had in mind at all. The winter was too cold, the growing season too short and most of the land too steep to farm. Despite all this, it turned out to be irresistible. There were ten buildings, on 450 acres and it even had its own small lake. Best of all for Vilayat, it had a small mountain from where he could look out on a wide expanse of the Hudson Valley, with the Catskill mountains lining the horizon. Right from the start he dreamed of living high up there.

The original plan to build on undeveloped land would have been impractical and most likely would have failed; the purchase was averted just in time. The fact that almost no one knew anything about farming or how to run a commune did not bother Pir Vilayat. He was always enthralled by the idea of bold experiments.

The first crew arrived on the property which Pir named the Abode of the Message in May 1975. Twenty pioneers took on the initial challenge of making the place habitable for the rest of us, plowing the farm to be and starting a garden which would hopefully supply food for the winter.

Not having been lived in for many years, the place was hardly livable. At least a hundred windows were broken and the heating systems needed replacing. Since most had come seeking refuge from the materialistic world, no one sought outside work, although funds were needed to support the community. Luckily there were a few materialists among us. One brought a complete VW repair business from Kansas. Another came with a tractor and a complete bakery from Philadelphia.

By summer's end over seventy members had moved in although few were artists or writers. Pir's vision for the Abode was forced to adjust to reality. He had hoped that it could support artists, writers, and craftsmen, but things clearly did not happen that way. We had to discover how to run and support the place by trial and error. This required many family meetings. At the start Pir sat through some of these interminable sessions, but they were thoroughly exhausting.

Gradually they were called much less often, and we saw less and less of him as he immersed himself in his writing.

Pir Vilayat first met Taj who was then a student of Murshid Sam at the Colorado camp. When he first saw her he said, "What's an angelic being like you doing on this planet?" Out of her mouth, without any thought came the words, "To be with you." Apparently there had been instant recognition; Vilayat believed that they were soul mates. It would soon become necessary for Taj to complete the separation from her estranged husband so as to be free to be with Pir Vilayat. Thus began a lifelong spiritual partnership joining their lives, in which they would together work to spread the teachings of Inayat Khan.

Vilayat and Taj had come to the Abode with their young son. Taj brought an important steadying influence to Vilayat's life. That and the love and support she gave him made all the difference during this otherwise difficult period. The schedule he took on soon became punishing, with three or four seminars every month which meant frequent flying. The demands on his time and energy were growing, along the stress of starting a new community. As a result, Taj soon assumed several important new roles, supporting him and his work as well as the community itself.

That first winter Vilayat, Taj and the children lived in what had originally been the first cabin built by an early pioneer in the wilderness. In 1789 at a revival meeting Henry Isaacs had been inspired when he heard Mother Ann Lee talk. He decided to join the Shakers and donated his farm for their first community. His tiny house had been rebuilt several times but not improved much. It had no insulation, no water and of course not even a toilet. Pir never complained. He was used to austerity, none of his caves had much in the way of amenities either.

Taj played a crucial part in making the community a success. Her common sense and calm presence had a balancing effect, while her classes and meditations greatly enhanced the spiritual presence.

She helped edit a new monthly publication of the Sufi Order

called *The Message,* which greatly helped tie together the growing number of students and served as a way Pir and others could spread the teachings as well as strengthen Pir's organization.

Many of these students were looking for ways they could serve the work. Through Amnesty International they joined Taj in publicizing the plight of political prisoners in an ongoing writing campaign to bring pressure on the authorities. Pir Vilayat said that helping political prisoners was also the work of his sister Noor-un-Nisa after her death. It was just one of the ways Taj served to enhance what Pir Vilayat was doing. Her skill in organizing is also apparent in both of the books he wrote in this period. I thought them the clearest and most readable of all that he would write. During this time she was also raising Zia, who was to become Pir Vilayat's successor, as well as their second son Mirza.

By the second year there were well over a hundred of us, far more than the buildings had been meant to hold. Initially everyone had different ideas on how things should be run, but of course no one had any actual community experience. That was a challenge, especially with our teacher a recluse who disliked rules. He had however, picked a fine manager. Under Stephan Rechtschaffen's direction the community managed to survive through what we called 'Operation Survival.'

Pir Vilayat was never attached to money and had a marked distrust of rich spiritual organizations. Perhaps as a result that was one problem we did not have. However as none of us wanted to go outside for work there was a lack of income to keep us going.

As soon as he could, Pir had a tiny room, lined with foam built for his use on the top floor of the main building. He hoped to find both quiet and warmth, both in short supply. At the time, he was working on what some believe would become his finest book, *The Message in Our Time,* an exploration and expansion of his father's teachings.

In a few years he had a bigger house built for his growing family, on a hill above the main village. He wanted the plaster on the walls put on rough to make it look more like a cave. That was as close as the resemblance ever got. It was too big for his taste by far.

I remember him saying, "Do you like big houses? I don't." His solution was to build a small hut perched on the hillside above it. It was big enough to hold two chairs, a small table for his computer, and a bright red telephone and matching red metal fireplace in the center. Later he would somehow add a sink and a shower. It was yurt shaped like his favorite hat and we began calling it Pir's pod.

When he was asked why he liked that shape, he answered without hesitation, "It's the blood of Genghis Khan in my veins." He repeated this on other occasions, rather proudly I thought.

I was long puzzled as to why he craved small spaces, rock enclosed if possible. The answer would finally come during one of his talks as he explained, "All the great Sufi masters and saints have attained power and majesty through very austere practice of the dhikr. Ab'il Khair did the dhikr enclosed in a niche in a wall. When you are enclosed in such a little place, you expand in another plane. He was the most powerful being you could imagine."

Pir was not one to accept limits as to what was possible. This was especially true in regards to consciousness itself. He said that it was even possible to enter into the minds of animals. Once when he complained about the mice in his pod, I suggested that he should try to convince them to live elsewhere. He said with some resignation, "I tried, but it didn't work." It was never clear whether the reason was because the mice could not be tempted with other accommodations, or because of the vast differences in levels of awareness. I could understand how hard it was for him to share the viewpoint of a mouse. The challenge posed by eagles would be far easier for such a master. It turned out that even if the mice would not move, the pod could, although it would never be as portable as a yurt, at least it could be transported. In a few years he put in a road and had it moved up on the mountain to a spot with a grand view. The road was a challenge itself at times, especially after rains or snow, which daunted even the most intrepid. Perhaps that was part of the reason he wanted to live there as he so loved solitude. For winter access he considered the possibility of an all terrain vehicle, but in the end he decided to use skis instead.

The pod was very much his work space, other functions like sleeping and eating were somehow accommodated, but they were in the nature of afterthoughts. He never needed to do much cooking as there were always willing volunteers to bring his simple meals up to him. Eventually he managed to put in a shelf which was just big enough for him to crawl up and sleep on, a little like the one he had in his Chamonix cave. Designing it required ingenuity, but he loved these kinds of challenges. The whole pod was hardly twelve feet in diameter which proved rather big for him, so he had a mini pod, half the size built next to it. Apart from being comfortably small, the mini pod freed him from the annoyance of a telephone. He suffered from the misfortune of being on call from two continents at different hours.

The mini pod was designed so everything in it could be reached with a turn of his swivel chair. It always amazed me how well he managed to function with books festooned with markers sticking out and papers all piled on top of one another. Perhaps there was a system of organization, but it was hard to see, well disguised as it was under all the clutter. From the outside his pod looked shabby as the many coats of white paint could not hide the patchwork of fiberglass applied over time. Unfortunately all these attempts to make it waterproof were only partially successful, and as a result it gradually rotted. Pir Vilayat was not overly bothered by this. His only attachments that I could see were to his cave in the Alps, his beggar's bowl, and his cello.

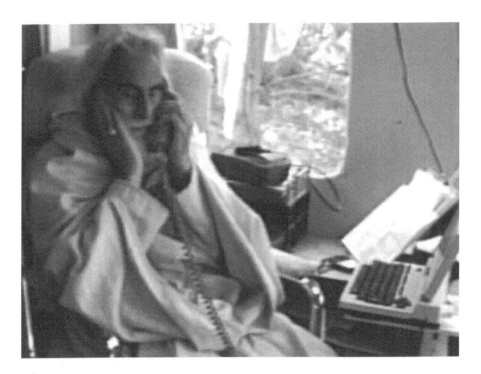

When he got his first laptop however, he was as excited as a small boy cutting and pasting away with a new toy. Before then, it all had to be done with scissors and pieces of paper which festooned all of his many books. Computers and printers were essential to him as no one could read his hand writing. On our way to India with Zia who wanted to study Buddhism, we stopped in Japan and while Zia and I visited temples, Pir spent his time looking for a new portable printer not yet available in the US. He got up in the middle of the night and wanted to try it. The only outlet was in the bathroom. I put it on the toilet seat but it fell and broke. I had to carry it around India without either of us being sure what language it would print.

Pir did better on his next pod which he built as an octagon and which stayed dry. It was next to his vacation cottage located outside the small village of Limoux in the Pyrenees, an hour's drive from the ancient walled city of Carcassonne well beyond the reach of telephones or even electricity. That also gave him a good excuse to design his own solar generators and water heater. Most of his shopping trips were in search of hardware to improve his latest improvements.

Apart from tinkering, he could spend his time here writing and training his latest eagle. Pir loved the challenge of this ancient art. What was required first was to build up the bird's confidence. Locking eyes with it, he would gradually come closer, thus slowly building up its trust. In my case it took time to build enough confidence to feel comfortable around either of them. When I made a mistake Pir's glance could be icy, while I found the eagle's stare awesome.

When Vilayat first learned the falconer's art he so valued freedom he tried to dispense with the thin leather strap tied to the bird's feet. As a result he lost several birds. In this way he realized that one must first practice the time honored rules before one can dispense with them. In the end, his Imperial eagle became so well trained he would follow along with the van and return when it was called.

Back home at the Abode Pir maintained his punishing schedule. When not giving talks or retreats he divided his time between Suresnes, the Abode and the summer Alps Camp, after which he would vacation in the Pyrenees. Even when he was at the Abode we often saw little of him. In his absence Taj was effectively the spiritual leader of the community. She led classes, gave counseling, and was tasked with dealing with personal conflicts within the community.

It often seemed to me that the Abode was more of a pressure cooker than a spiritual finishing school where large egos in close proximity were being heated, melted down and could thus hopefully be transformed. This naturally placed a heavy burden on Taj. While we could share ideas at family meetings, we had no mechanism to resolve conflicts, thus there was a tendency to ignore problems or to push them under the rug. This was a tendency that Pir Vilayat himself had inherited and was a problem that plagued other spiritual organizations as well.

The Sufi Order moved to Santa Fe in 1980 and Taj decided to move there herself. She told the story of how one day, while she was looking for a place to live, Pir pointed to a house on a hilltop and said, "What about that one?" The real estate agent told them, "It's not on the market, but I can ask." When she did, the owners replied, "We had not thought of selling, but since you suggest it, we might." They did. It was a magnificent Spanish-style, split-level house. Of course, from Pir's point of view, it was large, even larger than the last one, however, it sat high up with grand views of the desert.

Although our numbers had gradually been declining for some time, the departures increased as a number of Taj's students left to be with her in Sante Fe as well. In all we lost twenty people. Her absence was keenly felt. We clearly needed a resident teacher involved with the community. Pir was traveling much of the time so we saw less and less of him, although he loved his pod on the mountain and the Abode would remain his permanent home in the New World.

Chapter 8
THE MUSIC OF LIFE

Sound is the force that groups all things from atoms to worlds. The chording vibration sounds in all the innermost being of man and can only be heard in silence. When we go into the inner chamber and shut the door to every sound that comes from the life without, then the voice of God speaks to our soul and we will know the keynote of our life.
— HAZRAT INAYAT KHAN

The universe is like a symphony. The ultimate attunement is in the realm of emotion. One feels the emotion that moves the Universe, and that emotion will bring us in sync with the Cosmic Harmony.

The silent voice of the Divine Presence, the Divine Message, is whispered by all beings as they announce their names in their contribution to the symphony of the spheres.
— PIR VILAYAT INAYAT KHAN

Hazrat Inayat Khan was a pioneer in the use of sound as a spiritual instrument. From his years of musical studies he had also learned the art of attuning himself and others. Music was a part of Vilayat's life from the beginning. Some of his earliest memories were of his father singing to him. Later the whole family would sing the dhikr every evening. In this way their father would tune them, analogous to tuning an instrument. Pir Vilayat remembered it this way:

> I come from a musical family. My father Hazrat Inayat Khan was given the prize of Tansen of India, the highest prize that can be awarded to a musician, by the Nizam of Hyderabad. He later made the sacrifice of giving up music in order to bring the message of Sufism to the West. When you know what music meant to my

father, you realize what that sacrifice meant. Occasionally, in the early days, he would offer himself the luxury of singing and playing the vina. Later even that was not possible; there was no time.

I still remember the moment when he sung to us children. When I think of it now, I realize he was instructing us in music. He started with the more popular style of music, then he sang a semi-classical style. Finally he sang something very high and spiritual. He wanted us to feel the difference in the different styles. When he sang in the very high style, he was lost in meditation. He was actually communicating the message of spiritual life through music. People were entranced by the spiritual ecstasy he was communicating.

For Pir Vilayat music was a doorway to sacred realms. Inayat Khan once said it this way: "The true use of music is to become musical in one's thoughts, words and actions. Harmony is best given by producing harmony in one's own life."

Pir believed that his treasured cello had a soul, which had been formed by its owners and the music it had played over the centuries. Then one day someone knocked it over. Its soul was damaged, perhaps beyond repair. We shared in his pain.

He quoted his father as saying, "It is because music is the picture of the Beloved that we love music." "The way in which man can find· his own place is to tune his instrument to the keynote of the chord to which he belongs," and "Life is a symphony, and the action of every person in this symphony is the playing of his part, his particular part in this music." Pir explained how the Indian musician would tune himself by tuning his instrument. Gradually one learns how to feel when the sound is just right and become more sensitive and "feel with the heart." He urged us to do the same when intoning mantras. Here is another passage he liked to quote from his father that explains why this is so:

> What we call music in our everyday language is only a miniature which our intelligence has grasped of that music or harmony of the whole universe which is working behind everything and which is the source and origin of nature... The music of the universe is the background of the small picture which we call music. Our sense of music, our attraction to music, shows that there is music in the depth of our being. What does music teach us? Music helps
>
> train us in harmony. Man, being a miniature of the universe, shows harmonious and inharmonious chords. Vibrations can be changed by understanding one's life, understanding the rhythm of the mind.
>
> The soul of music is the sound itself. The musician or composer paints with all the tones of the various instruments or voices. The quality of the resulting vibrations is all important, since they affect our body, mind, and soul just as they have an effect on the atoms of the musical instrument.
>
> The musician creates a beautiful sound by becoming one with his instrument. To create a lovely tone he uses the current of his breath.

This is especially true for singing and wind instruments, but even the violinist or the drummer employs the current of his breath imparted to the instrument through his hands. The tone produced depends on the shape of what produces it, round bodies produce more mellow tones with more weight and depth, while narrow shapes produce more penetrating tones. The converse is when we are more receptive, we become empty like the hollow reed which can receive the divine breath.

Hazrat Inayat Khan wrote, "The effect of music depends not only on the proficiency but also the evolution of the performer. He who gradually progresses along the path of music in the end attains to the highest perfection. No other art can inspire and sweeten the personality like music." Gradually one becomes ever more sensitive and until one reaches the point when one begins to hear the inner sounds.

Murshid had described ten inner sounds similar to sounds in the world. In the earlier years Pir used these descriptions but there came a time when he began to describe them differently, based it seemed on his own rather than his father's experience. He called it the "Unheard Music" which one can only perceive when in harmony with it. Pir compared this to what one might hear if one were able to hear the sounds of atoms vibrating, a bit like a wind harp. He said that at some point one should let oneself begin to dissolve and hopefully, "perceive oneself as a body of vibration." Hopefully we might then be able to hear more and more of what he also called "The Universal Sound heard within," which he said was like perceiving "the vibrational patterns of a crystal."

These inner sounds were the Music of the Spheres first described by Pythagoras who thought that musical harmony was the key to understanding the laws of the universe. To perceive it required extensive tuning of one's own instrument. Here is how Pir explained the process:

> As you keep on tuning into the sound you become more and more harmonious, more and more impersonal....work with the sound until you are absolutely amazed that you could produce such a sound and it seems that you are just the instrument through which the Divine piper blows the whisper of the incantations of its magic spell.

At a certain stage it seems as though you are picking up not only the overtones, or even the echoes of the vibrations, but the response of the beings whose particular wave lengths one has stirred. After practicing the wazifa listen to the harmonics, climb the ladder of the harmonics, become yourself pure vibration, float on the sea of vibration; you are in the absolute inner sound. You can do it if you identify yourself with pure vibration.

While Pir Vilayat's knowledge of music was vast, his tastes were very selective. Over the years he had put together a special collection of choral works. Much of this was music of invocation, praise, and glorification. Pir believed it reflected the angelic nature of the soul. Its effect when I first heard it was overwhelming. I had never suspected that music like this existed. Just imagine what the effect of hearing music like this throughout one's life would be. For example Victoria's *Lamentations of Jeremiah* was sung in every cathedral in Europe for the final days of Holy Week during the Renaissance. When he composed it in the monastery of Montserrat, Tomás Luis de Victoria was under the guidance of the saint Philip Neri.

Pir believed that the great composers of that age were on the leading edge of evolution in their time, and that their music must have had profound effect on the whole of Europe. This was a time when most music was choral and all choral music was still sacred. From that point on, Western civilization has gradually lost touch with its sacredness. In the process Pir along with Carl Jung believed it increasingly lost touch with its own soul.

In Pir's mind Bach clearly towered above all other composers. He felt that his music constituted a kind of depiction of the Divine Order. He loved to recite from memory how Bach had described it. :

> The art of my science, the science of my art no one but me knows. I am trying to create an example of a human commonwealth. For each theme an instrument, for each instrument a theme, not an autocratic imposition of one theme upon the others, as in a melody with accompaniment, but each theme contributing organically towards the richness of the whole, each one restricting its freedom by imposing self-discipline upon itself in the interest of the whole.

It was in this music that Pir Vilayat said one could best experience aspects of the Divine Emotion so hard to find in other music. Here he one description he wrote:

> I always regard Bach as being a spiritual master, in the hierarchy of masters, who used the language of music. The High Mass of Bach played such a great part in my thinking. As I had gone so deeply into that experience during those months when I was listening to it every evening, you can imagine what that was like for me. The great moment is when there is the wailing of the crucifixion, going into the depths of human suffering. Then all of a sudden, it breaks with such a tremendous freedom, it's fantastic. This is important because the most powerful thing that can happen to us is when we experience resurrection, the overcoming of suffering and the unleashing of the forces of joy.

One of the few other piece of music that had affected him as deeply was the *Miserere* by Gregorio Allegri. This is what he told us:

> The Miserere by Allegri represents the very highest expression of music ever. The pope and the cardinals only allowed it to be played once a year, on Ash Wednesday, in the Sistine Chapel of the Vatican. Over a century after its composition, Mozart heard it and was able to write the whole thing down from memory. It's one of the most heart-rending pieces I know.

Pir often spoke of the power of ecstasy. The best way he could share that was through music. For the subtlest expressions of ecstasy he would play certain Sufi music for us. He explained it this way:

> What is the power of the dervish? What is really the essential power of Sufism? It's the power of ecstasy. The reason the dervish has such a strong attraction for you is that he is in a state of intoxication. Anything that makes you lose your confinement in your ego-consciousness and makes you feel greater than yourself, that's what ecstasy is. It's discovering the divine emotion behind everything that happens in the whole universe. The greatest ecstasy is discovering the Divine Emotion. This is so powerful that you can never be the same after you've experienced it.

His favorite was the Syrian singer and poet Abed Azrie, whose poems set to music Pir liked to use for whirling. It had what he called "the ecstasy of sobriety," filled with the pain of longing:

> We must not confuse ecstasy with joy, although it sounds very much like it. It's something else: there's a combination of joy and pain in it. It's the joy that arises out of the broken heart. So the ecstasy of the Sufi, the intoxication of the Sufi, comes from his particular type of wine. The dervish says, "If I can't dance, what can I do?" Intoxication is a state in which one participates in the dance of Shiva — and yet the highest intoxication, curiously enough, is sobriety. That's peace instead of joy.

Just as it took a Rumi to capture such exquisite emotions in words, only the very finest musicians could manage to fully express them. Pir's favorite was Shahram Nazeri, singing poems of Rumi. Some of the words were:

> Listen to the unstruck sounds,
> and what sifts through that music.
> Listen within your ear
> Speak without forming words.
> Language turns against itself.

Besides having mastery, the performer had to be an empty vessel himself. It was helpful to have a receptive audience, which could inspire him so that the spirit could flow unimpeded. For this reason such music was usually performed in small intimate settings. The magic of Pir's presence could make it happen almost anywhere, but the spirit itself seemed to prefer uplifting locations, just as he did.

Over the years Pir collected a great deal of music for use with his meditations and retreats. He was constantly coming up with new ideas for which we needed more music. This gave me a new mission which was to visit music stores as we traveled. Toronto, London, Paris and Delhi, turned out to be the best, but my search even took me behind the Iron Curtain as well as to Bombay where I was able to some get rare Zoroastrian chants from the head priest there. Finding music for him became my passion as well as my mission. It was especially rewarding when I discovered music that really pleased him

In time we collected selections for all the planets, planes, elements, chakras, and, as well as for every stage of the retreat. For astral music Pir used the ephemeral Debussy *Clair de Lune*. Surprisingly he chose some electronic music which he felt had a fine jinn quality, quick and unpredictable. He used Slavic chants for sacredness, majesty, and peace. The highest planes were all beyond form, which meant that at that level they were beyond sound as we know it I wondered how any music could correspond to these. That never seemed to bother Pir, as long as the emotions felt right, he knew that music might help lift us up there. Finding the right music gave him a creative challenge that he loved. In the process we could discover new levels of sacredness and exquisite emotions we might never have experienced otherwise.

One of Pir's many inspirations was the idea of pairing music with appropriate wazifas. This also gave him a way to share some of his favorite classical pieces. He wanted to help us to experience the meaning of these mantras beyond words. At times he would use Beethoven symphonies or Brahms concertos as well as his favorite Arvo Pärt.

One of the more striking pieces he played was the Bach Concerto for Four Harpsichords, which he used for whirling. I thought this a far better choice than the traditional Turkish Whirling Dervish music. Just imagine, had Rumi been able to hear it, people might be whirling in concert halls today!

Pir loved to conduct, although he was never trained to do it. Once Newell Jenkins, who was a professional conductor, tried to improve his technique. He stood behind him and moved Pir's arms; Pir accepted this quite humbly. No doubt Newell's technique was better, but he could not compare with Pir in imbuing the music with feeling. For Vilayat the point of great music was not just enjoyment, but to feel it so deeply that one might be tuned and transformed by it. When conducting, Pir brought out the full gamut of emotion he wanted it to express. He did this with his whole being, not just with his hands and arms, but his mouth and eyes, every part of him became tools in the process. He would crouch low, and then stand on his toes as the music swelled. This was not so much conducting as it was willing forth emotions in the performers with the power of his being.

What an experience it was to sing in the choir then, or even just watching him! He told us his ambition was to conduct a choir of angels. But as he ruefully admitted, "No doubt this stemmed from some purely personal ambition of mine."

Watching how willing he was to learn from Newell, or playing his cello despite many wrong notes was a teaching in itself. He seemed to be totally free from any self-consciousness to a degree I had never imagined possible. All that mattered at these moments was sharing the emotion. This was just one of many other ways he managed to share exalted emotions with us.

He said it was his music teachers who had the deepest impact of all for him. First of course was his father, but next came Nadia Boulanger. Most important was what she taught him about creativity as well as how to inspire others. This was the essence of the art of teaching itself. He would use what he learned to teach teachers in years to come.

Pir Vilayat attributed his sweet cello tone to what he had learned from Pablo Casals. Pir told us how profoundly moving it had been to listen to him practice. Those hours he spent had no doubt deepened his understanding of Bach as well. Casals' appreciation of Bach was second to none. Casals would never release any of his later recordings of the Bach's cello suites after those he did during the period when Vilayat was there listening to him practice.

Dance was another way he loved to tune us. With dance he could share more of his favorite music at the same time. Here was one of the rare times he felt free of his role as the teacher. Dancing for him had to be spontaneous and free form. Perhaps this explained why he never used the dances created by Murshid Sam. Perhaps they were too structured for him; what a pity! They could have complemented what he was doing, and we all loved them.

When he danced with us, Pir's joy was infectious, as was his boundless energy. How else could he keep us all at it for an hour or more? I would get so exhausted that I would beg him to stop, even though he was more than twenty years older than I was. Years later when we talked frankly, he explained he thought that the reason was that I did not like Bach!

Listening to music with Pir could be an extraordinary experience.

It certainly seemed that we were hearing with his ears, and perhaps even feeling what he was feeling. Time and again people I would hear people say, "It's never the same when I hear it by myself." The magic of his presence could take us where no words could reach. At times his pleasure was as infectious as a small child's joy. He was also constantly finding new outlets for his creative urges. One wonders what music he would have written had he been a composer, or in what direction his genius would have taken him as an inventor or as scientist. He said, "Creativity is the thrust of ecstasy and makes it an actuality in our lives. The mantras he loved the best and choose for creativity were: What if? And aha!"

Pir Vilayat even created his own theatrical production, a pageant of music and drama which would eventually be performed in a cathedral and a stadium. Here is how he explained its origin:

> I remember, it was at Easter, we had organized a retreat and I had been leading a meditation on light, and when I opened my eyes and looked at people I thought, "They don't seem to be any more luminous than before. I have failed." And I thought: "What am I doing? If it doesn't have a real effect on people, what is the point of meditating on light and thinking of light and talking about light if it doesn't really mean something?" I must say, it was one of those moments in my life when I went through a kind of crisis, like Gandhi when he said, "I have failed."
>
> But that evening, we were going to a Catholic church for midnight mass and everybody said, "Couldn't we just celebrate mass together?" And I said, "I don't know how to celebrate mass, and anyway, I would not be authorized to do it, but still…" Finally, we did it. At the end we were dancing with candles around the altar, and there was light in everybody's eyes and I thought, "Now, look at that!"

Not too long after, he had another inspiration when he attended an ecumenical meeting in Ohio. Here is his account:

> During the seventies there were teachers of different movements who were inspiring large numbers of people. One day, we were all invited to the Monastery of the Sacred Heart in Ohio. At one point in this gathering, all the teachers came

together to celebrate their worship together. It was incredible –
all these spiritual leaders who normally never would have met
before, and who sometimes criticized each other's teachings,
joined in what I would call a cosmic celebration.

It was my life's dream; something that I had always longed
for. Something was coming through at that moment in time;
it was as if for one brief moment, we had opened the doors
between the physical world and the celestial spheres. What
came through in our acts of glorification was a reminiscence of
the celestial spheres and of that original state of innocence that
we still find in the child within.

Out of these experiences the 'Cosmic Celebration' emerged. He
wanted to enact on an earthly stage something of the celebrations
in the heavens. What he had in mind was a great pageant bringing
together the prophets and founders of all the world's religions, as well
as angelic beings arrayed on each of the higher planes as described
in the Kabbalah. Fittingly, it would be staged in the great Episcopal
cathedral of Saint John the Divine in New York.

The Universal Worship had been his father's great inspiration,
which like any form, could stagnate without growth and change.
But adding whole religions was not something he undertook lightly.
After much soul searching he agreed to adapt it to the times by
introducing the divine feminine as well as the native religions.
What mattered to him was that we could experience the Spirit and
some of the glory of the Heavens. There were times when he held
services without an altar under difficult conditions, but what was
never missing was the Spirit itself. In many ways I was reminded of
the determination of Teilhard de Chardin also saying mass without
an alter or even a candle, still obedient to the church which had
banned his writings and effectively banished him to remote places
in China.

During the Universal Worship services Pir's genius for theater
came out. With his presence and in the music he played for us, he
could transmit divine qualities in ways that we could feel, especially
glorification, majesty and joy but most important was the sacredness.

In helping us to experience these he aways hoped to thus put us in touch with those same qualities we had within but which were still latent and thus help them to manifest.

Of all my memories, I think my fondest is singing the "Hallelujah" set to the melody of the Pachelbel Canon, at the end of retreats. It would be a perfect ending to what we already had experienced and helped us to end on a note of jubilation. On the occasions when we sung it after his death, some of the feeling was still there, but the difference was so very apparent.

Chapter 9
THE MASTERS

There is a mind behind all minds; there is a heart which is the source of all hearts; there is a spirit that collects and accumulates all the knowledge that every living being has had. No knowledge or discovery that has ever been made is lost. It all accumulates and collects in that mind as an eternal reservoir.

— PIR VILAYAT INAYAT KHAN

Pir Vilayat was able to bring the masters, saints and prophets alive for us. As he stood before the altar invoking Melchizedek he would seem to become larger and more majestic and we felt the essence of that great being. When he played music of the crucifixion we could all feel some of Christ's agony with him. What I began to realize was just how very accessible these beings must have been to him. Although he would never make any such claims, one realized that when he spoke of the masters he was speaking from a kind of direct experience.

One Halloween at the Abode in 1976, Pir Vilayat devoted an entire evening to the different masters. When someone asked him if he could tells us what Murshid was like at that time. Here is what he said:

> I can only say what I experience myself when I try to contact him. He looks somewhat as he used to look, but a little different too. His hair is totally white and there is much more of it. The sense of suffering that one felt doesn't seem to be there. He's very optimistic and very much in charge. His aura is glistening white although there seems to be a lot of colors coming out of it. He is in a cathedral of light which is in a certain sense an extension of his body, or generated out of his soul. Sometimes it looks a bit like a crystal palace, but when you go more deeply into it you see

that it's not solid in any way. He is surrounded by whole galaxies of beings who are all working in the same direction. Although in one sense I don't think there is a location of his being, at the same time I feel there is some kind of location around Jupiter's moon, Io, which scientists are very interested in at present because it has many unusual features. That's as much as I can say.

However, over the years he did tell us other things about his father. At one point he said, he was helping to bring advanced souls to this planet where they were greatly needed. At another time he explained to us that Murshid was working with leaders of the different religions, especially the Russian Orthodox Church. Here was another account:

Well, suppose we could listen to the dervishes very closely. Hazrat Inayat Khan will say: Can you see the right in what appears to be wrong, and the wrong in what appears to be right? Can you see the success in what seems to be a catastrophe or the catastrophe that seems to you to be a success? Can you see the meaningfulness where there is the appearance of total confusion? Can you see disorder behind the order that people establish? Can you see the cause behind the cause, behind the cause? ..... Can you discover in your consciousness the very consciousness of the Universe?

When someone else asked him about Serapis then great Egyptian master, he answered in the following words:

Serapis is a master of vibration, he is regulating the sound relationships between the planets, like the notes in a symphony. He's essentially embodied in the symphony of the spheres, and is much more concerned with planetary phenomena than with working at the human level. He works with all kinds of waves, radio waves, X-rays, gamma rays, and the intelligence manifesting in vibrations, which is the intelligence behind the whole universe. He is a very fine expression of the divine intelligence; he doesn't have much love. He's extremely speedy, fast, moving like the wind, and totally unpredictable. Where there's an emergency, he strikes with great surety and dexterity. He functions mainly at the jinn level, influencing the genius of men, especially scientists.

Someone asked, "Could you say something about the archangel Michael?" Pir replied:

> Michael represents the knighthoods in the universe, the militia of people who have definitely dedicated themselves to fight for the victory of light over darkness, or righteousness over deception.
>
> There are many different temperaments among people. If for example you are born with a very strong feeling that you must help to heal people and relieve suffering in the world, that means that your inheritance from the archangel Raphael is stronger than from any other archangel. If you are born with a natural tendency to make reforms, you carry an inheritance from the archangel Gabriel. If you're born as a real knight or warrior dedicated to fighting against injustice as Noor fought in the Second World War, standing for what is right and protecting the weak from the terrible scourge of Nazism, then you are dedicated to Michael.
>
> Michael and Gabriel are a little different but are very close. Gabriel is always connected to the Message, bringing reform, a new way of organizing life, a new form of society, a new dispensation. That's why he always appears to the messengers. He appeared to Muhammad; he was the one who brought the Holy Spirit to the Virgin Mary; he appeared to Zoroaster in the form of Vohu Manu.
>
> Michael represents more of the fighting knight, rather than the reformer.

When Pir Vilayat was asked to talk about the master Saint Germain, he said:

> He has appeared at different times in history. One of those was as Rakoczy, a Hungarian. He's very elusive, intervening in a mysterious way, most often in politics. He usually appears when there is a real crisis. Quite rightly he is expected to appear again on the planet at this particular time because there actually is a crisis brewing.
>
> Saint Germain works with light and insight, flummoxing the adversary with his surprising insight, exposing the bad faith of people, and giving the sudden realization of the "I am," the words in the burning bush, bringing about a totally new realization of one's identity. His vision is like a landfall in the message of our time, a totally new way of looking upon 'I.'

At that point Pir said it was presumptuous for him to speak about female saints or masters and he asked Taj to do so. Here is what she said:

In a woman the attribute of power is different from what one would normally think. To encounter this I suggest the being of Hazrat Babajan, who is a lady dervish. Her power is an uncompromising dedication to the divine presence. Her presence gives me the same feeling as doing dhikr. In fact she is the dhikr.

Another woman who should be mentioned is St Teresa of Avila, a nun who lived at the time of St John of the Cross, in Spain. She was both a very deep mystic and very practical at the same time. The purpose behind her life was to convey the realization that is entrusted to the mystic and her experience of communion with God to the nuns she was working with.

It was this unique combination of deep mystical revelation which grows out of intense love of God, together with utter simplicity and thoughtfulness in dealing with the details of a life of prayer, which allows her writing to be a continual source of inspiration to people of all times who have embarked with sincerity upon a life of prayer. While the depth of her soul is immersed in the mystery of God, she is busy helping her fellow nuns to live the life of the spirit. Her total lack of pretense while imparting such deep revelations endears her readers to her in a special way.

There's another woman who is very veiled; that is, she doesn't come out of the silent life enough to be recognized. One has to enter into that world in order to come into contact with her. On earth she was Bibi Hafiz Jamal, the daughter of Moinuddin Chishti, and she is continually in a state of prayer. As with the other women masters and saints, she is deeply attuned to the aspect of the divine presence, which is the being of God.

Therefore, prayer and the quality of holiness come through very strongly in her, because she is moved by the incredible meaning of God's gift of himself to creatures and what that involves. Through that gift comes the divine presence and in response to the act of giving, one feels the sense of sacredness; and then one wishes to become the guardian of that Presence. So naturally the aspect of prayer then becomes important, and Bibi Hafiz Jamal epitomizes the very essence of prayer.

Chapter 10
ANGELS AND JINNS

Mankind is clothed in the garb of an angel, of a jinn, and of a human being; but when he only sees himself in the garb of a human being without seeing the other garbs, he believes he is nothing but a human being.
— HAZRAT INAYAT KHAN

Our concepts of the angels owe much to the Zoroastrian religion. Zoroaster taught that each person has a *fravashi* who guides and protects him. Hazrat Inayat Khan and Pir Vilayat used some of these traditional concepts of angels, but went much further. What Pir told us was clearly not just based on his father's ideas, but on his own insight and actual experience. He said:

> There are two types of angels; those who remain on the angelic planes and have never incarnated, and those who have. Angels gather wisdom by incarnating. The Sufis distinguish between the two. The first are called *fereshta*, the second are *malik* and *hur*, that is where the word *hurkalya* which means "a city in the heavens" comes from. There are those who are only passing through the angelic planes and are on their way down, as we have been, and others who are on their way up from their physical condition.
>
> As the soul descends it collects the atoms of radiance of the angelic planes. The spirit that has the greater power can reach right down to the earth plane, because on the earth plane there is a fullness of experience that is necessary for the unfoldment of their being. There are some beings who shy away from it and remain on the angelic planes. There are of course children who die early, who have overshot the mark, and they are shocked by conditions as they see them, and are permitted then to return to their original abode. In the human condition one thinks one is experiencing something, but in the angelic plane the universe does the experiencing. In the

human condition one thinks one understands something, but here it is the divine mind that does the understanding. As the angels have no guile, they see things with the clarity of the disarming truthfulness of the innocent. Murshid said, "The relation of angels to human beings is as that of a little child to a grown-up person; they can help human beings as an infant can help its elders."

The angels are described as beings of light. It's a different kind of light, just as there is a difference between the light of your consciousness and the light of your aura. The best way to describe the fabric of the angelic bodies is to say they seem like ethereal interwoven meshes of light, and simultaneously high-frequency waves of vibration. When you are in a airplane with the sun rising above the clouds it is very reminiscent of the angels floating above those landscapes of light.

Pir Vilayat also stressed that we have angelic components to our being and how important it is to experience these higher aspects in our selves:

Can you imagine a being whose light is more radiant than the sun? That is an archangel. You carry the inheritance of that being. Once you have established your connection with the being of the sun, rather than just the light, then you have access to further and further beings of light, to cosmic beings of light. But it is not good enough to just try to contact a being, one must experience oneself as that being. The light that you are includes the hierarchies of beings of light.

Remember of course that the aura of a person is part of the aura of the planet earth and the aura of the earth is part of the aura of the sun, which is part of the aura of the greater sun, and so on. In the same way we have angelic as well as arch angelic components to our being. What I thought was my light is the light of the archangel, of whose aura my light is an atom in his light, and he derives his light from the light of the archangel above him. There is the archangel of the planet earth and the archangel of the solar system and an archangel of the galaxy. Each one is hierarchically above the other, and each one derives his light from the one above him.

You can recognize an angelic being on the earth plane because he or she is very loving and ready to help and is always attracted to that which is beautiful and true, and is a very harmonious being.

They are continually vibrating in a harmonious way. Of course, it is certainly true that the angelic beings that have been exposed to conditions on earth may be a little less harmonious, but as Hazrat Inayat Khan says the symphony is so vast that there is even room for disharmony in the symphony.

Some angels do communicate with people. It's generally angels who have already lived on the earth and they are seen in human garments or speak the language of people, but that is the way in which we find accommodation for them. Angels can experience the human condition through human minds. When that is done by a spirit on the astral plane, then it is called obsession.

A guardian angel is often an angel who did incarnate as a human being at some time and is now returned to the angelic state. Imagine that you have returned to the angelic state after having been a human, and you remember all your connections with people on the earth plane. You would naturally be concerned, and want to protect them against danger. The guardian angel is a being who is connected and has a protective feeling toward you and who comes either in emergency to protect you against accident or to guide you if he feels that you are making a mistake.

There are two forms of guidance, there is the guidance from the masters and the guidance from the angels; the difference between the two is that the masters have wisdom and the angels have ecstasy. Hopefully the master has ecstasy and wisdom too. If you are guided by an angel it will make you very high, but will not necessarily give you wisdom. Many people hear the call of those angelic spheres, it's a kind of homesickness. It is that call which will preserve you from the impressions of the earth. One thinks of it as protection from accidents, but it also gives protection from evil. That's the meaning of a guardian angel.

Angels are not the same as what we call spirits, who are beings not yet risen to the angelic level, and who are still in the nether world or in limbo between the two. Spirits try to contact beings on the physical plane because they are lonely; they haven't found their way and they are attached. The guardian angel is someone who is released. It's not out of attachment that he or she wants to contact you, but it's really because of a sense of responsibility towards you. You often find that it might have been a teacher for example, someone who is concerned about you. It's possible to have several guardian angels.

Pir clearly felt more at home in the angelic planes than in the jinn planes. Once when asked about the latter he answered that he could not say very much about these as he tended to pass right through these planes. However, it soon became apparent that he knew quite a bit about them. Pir explained that we have jinn as well as angelic components to our beings. Here is one account he gave:

The spirit which has become invested with atoms of angel bodies on descending into the jinn plane and has to adopt a body made up of the atoms of what you could say is the jinn body. Typically one sees it in the genius. The word is connected to the Sanskrit *jnana* meaning knowledge. The jinn mind is quick and always trying to understand; it will be attracted to art and music; philosophers and composers are among this type.

Pir Vilayat seemed to me to be a good example of someone with much jinn influence in his own being. Another time when he talked of jinns, he gave the impression that he was able to both perceive and communicate with them. Here is what he said:

Just as the outlines of the jinns are less distinctive than humans, the outlines of angels are even less distinct, as it is pure radiance, but the size is much greater.

The emotions of the angels are much more peaceful and much more remote, but luminous. Jinns may communicate with humans more frequently than angels. Jinns are also able to communicate with souls returning from the earth. It happens that jinns are sent to the earth with a mission, like angels. Of their own accord however, most jinns will not descend to the earth plane, because they are much happier where they are.

Both jinns and angels "die" at some point. The life span of the jinn is longer than that of the human and that of the angel is longer than the jinn. At the time of death they are absorbed into a higher condition.

Chapter 11
THE SPIRITUAL GOVERNMENT
OF THE WORLD

The whole universe has contributed to the way humanity thinks today. If the planet did not have an intelligence, it could not have intelligent beings on it. The collective working of several minds and the activity of the whole world in one direction are governed by the intelligence of the planet. The divine mind is completed after manifestation.
— HAZRAT INAYAT KHAN

Pir Vilayat explained that he had first begun to learn about the nature of the spiritual hierarchy from the rishis in India. He said:

> There is a Spiritual Government of the World, including non-incarnate beings. It is a hierarchy, which means that some people have a higher rank than others, like a government. Only a small fraction of them are known to all. The more one is conscious of one's vocation in ensuring the divine order in chaos, the more one is connecting with the government on the physical plane. They are not in different places, because there is no location, but they have their areas of control, and there is communication on this high level.
>
> Just imagine what this means: there is a whole invisible network behind our affairs, and you must never think that you are alone because you are always taken in charge by beings, who may appear very suddenly. ..... I was walking once somewhere in a village. A car had stopped and all of a sudden there was a dervish who came right up to me. You would not expect a dervish there. He communicated something and he was off again.

Hazrat Inayat Khan explained that there are levels of masters. The Pir is the lowest member in incarnation. His job is "to help individuals in the unfoldment of their souls." Above him is the Buzurg whose influence is wider. Next comes the Wali who harmonies all beings under his influence. Above him is the Ghaus who can give protection to a whole country. Above him is the Qutb, who is generally the highest master on Earth, although on occasion there may also be the Nabi, that is a prophet.

When asked about how one connects with a master, Pir answered, "You have to communicate with them in a whole different way." "It is generally through a being who has a connection with a being, who is connected with a being in the hierarchy." Pir explained that this is the meaning behind Christ's words "No man comes to the father except through me." In answer to the question as to whether there was a risk of interrupting a master who might be busy at the time, Pir responded:

> No, it doesn't matter. By definition the master should be able to be conscious at all times. For example he could be talking while at the same time receiving an SOS. I don't say that's always what happens, but that's what the master is supposed to do. The fact is that the masters who are dis-incarnate are pretty busy too. In fact even more busy. It doesn't prevent one from being able to contact them. Sometimes one has the feeling that they have an answering system that can register the problem so that they can deal with it a little later.
>
> It's amazing how concerned the masters are about the smallest details. They don't get annoyed if you ask them about details, but often they pass it back and say, "You have to work that out." They have to use your mind to reach you, so you are limiting their thoughts by your mind. Intuition consists in not allowing your mind to stand in the way of what is coming through. Unfortunately, we do use our minds, so we are continually limiting the message through our understanding. In addition, in order to experience the condition of the planets, they must use our minds. For general purposes they can feel the atmosphere, but for things like the nuclear disaster at Three Mile Island, they have to use your eyes.
>
> Since we are limiting their view by our eyes, then they have to make decisions based on the strength of what you see, they will always answer in more general terms. They will talk about the principles involved, but you have to work it out on earth. Also they do have to take into account your freedom, so they don't just tell you what to do. But if it's an emergency they have to act.

Hazrat Inayat Khan wrote,

> One person can save the world and one person can ruin it. That
> is only on the outer plane, in the spiritual plane the effect is still
> more powerful, only those who work on the spiritual plane do not
> manifest to view. What happens in the political world is known,
> but in the spiritual world great things happen and they are not
> known.

Baba Sita Ramdas Omkarnath was an example of another master
who functioned here on earth, and may have provided critical protection
for India. According to Pir:

> When there was danger of a war with China, he was at the
> border between India and China. When there was danger of
> a war between India and East Pakistan (Bangladesh), he was
> at the frontier. Now he is at the frontier between Pakistan and
> Afghanistan. He is always in the danger area, and he's always in
> samadhi. When you think about gurus, that is a real one: no ego
> there, and the power! He was just pure spirit; it wasn't human
> power, it was pure spirit, the power of God coming through him.
> It was incredible!

Pir once told us that the Hierarchy was moving towards more
synarchy. The dictionary defines synarchy as meaning ' to rule jointly.'
He explained it in terms of more input from below. This was long before
the Internet would empower individuals and small groups everywhere.
It was a good example of how events on Earth are initiated, as well as
part of processes jointly taking place on higher planes. However such
empowerments might equally be used by the Me Too Movement against
sexual harassment, or by hackers bent on subverting governments.

In 1975 Pir Vilayat gave an advanced class to a small group of
students in California, where he talked about the Spiritual Government
of the World in considerable depth. Here are some excerpts:

> We owe it to the well being of humanity to reestablish
> communication with the spiritual government of the World.
> Our responsibility is staying on the planet and making it

possible for the masters to reach us, instead of just reaching beyond ourselves. The government can only function if people will take heed of what it is trying to do, and they are only too happy when there is someone ready to respond. On the other hand, the government can only reveal its strategy to people who are able to understand it and who are also able to keep a secret.

You don't think that things just happen like that, without being prepared. There is planning, and the planning keeps on moving ahead. But it's not like everything is preplanned. The planning has to take into account people's freedom. It is like the planning of a composite being, called the Spiritual Government of the World. One must develop the ability to enter into the consciousness of those beings who are aware of the direction things are supposed to take. In attuning to particular masters we strengthen those qualities or aspects in ourselves, and of course in so doing, further the work of The Hierarchy.

Gradually one becomes incorporated into what we call the Spiritual Government of The World. Your domain is as wide as the influence of your soul; the higher the soul is attuned, the greater the awareness and the greater the domain. In the very high ranks you have beings who play a very important part in giving a sense of direction of humanity.

He explained that although we can think of the masters as having different functions, they also have their own areas of responsibility.

The lowest of all ranks is the Pir who is just responsible for a community of people, or an order which kind of reflects the divine order; actually a very poor replica of the Divine Order of course. It's a kind of karmic responsibility for people, it's giving people a sense of direction; it's assuming responsibility and protecting them from themselves sometimes.

Each of us has some kind of connection with the Hierarchy but it generally is through a being who is in contact with another being whom is contact with a being in the Hierarchy. Lower beings are in contact with higher beings, and so on, all of whom are members of the Spiritual Hierarchy of The World. When we say world, well it's a very big world. Like there are some who are in charge of the planet Earth. There are those who are in charge of not just Earth but perhaps of other planets, and others who are in charge of solar systems and galaxies and so on.

There are sometimes disagreements in the government. He said:

> Not like wars but real storms. The masters, saints and prophets each have their own line, yet there is a merging. Do you know that the masters are continually merging into one another? They can't even distinguish themselves from each other at times. When you are all beings, then you are all Masters and all Prophets and you are in the plants and in the animals and the minerals. You can merge into the consciousness of all beings. That means sharing their emotions, experiencing the vastness of their realizations, being a flame upon a light or a vibration upon a vibration. ....
>
> You will start experiencing a cathedral of light and the thunderbolts of lights which are the illuminated beings. There you can experience the power of the being that has become Truth, who has become as sensitive as a fine wire, and as strong as the truth of the universe, incorporating the consciousness of all beings into his consciousness. His heart has become as vast as the universe. That is the way you reach the master; not in his person but in his soul.
>
> Do you know how beings are related together in humanity? It's just like the seed and then the plant, over and over again. In the seed are the total qualities of the plant. So the soul of humanity that is the prophet, the messenger, is like the seed that contains within it the whole essence of humanity. He represents humanity, and as he passes to the other plane, part of his being proliferates into many beings.....then he reappears again in another form.
>
> Then you begin to realize the awe-inspiring reality that is inherent in the whole forward march of humanity. The heart of the whole network of the hierarchy of masters, saints, and prophets is continually working in all its branches, doing just one thing: spurring people on to the purpose of creation, which is awakening. Every being is longing for the day when he will awaken, and the entire being which is the Universe is gradually awakening. Every part of the One Being is also undergoing a process of awakening as part of the general awakening.
>
> We can say that the next step in the further human advancement is developing intuition. It is only this intuition that will give one access to the thinking of the officers of the Spiritual Government of the World. In order for The Government to achieve its purpose, there must be those who can receive its guidance and understand its purpose.

At one point he asked Taj to talk. Here are some excerpts:

The unfoldment of beings on earth is continually watched by beings hierarchically above us; the objective is to foresee and warn us of pitfalls, to spur us to overcome our limitations, to give us insight into our purpose, and to inspire us to take the next step. But the only way they can achieve this, as they can't speak to most beings directly, nor do most beings have access to a teacher who is a mouthpiece for the hierarchy, is to bring some person on earth to say what they wish to be said..

There is a gravity law about inspiration which is able to come through from a higher place into the heavy atmosphere of earth and earth-bound people: guidance tends to get distorted even by the mental atmosphere of the earth, and also of course by the one who receives it. That person has to adjust his thinking to it, but he also exercises some influence on the inspiration, so that he gets a flattened version of something which is really multidimensional. It has already been badly distorted before reaching human ears.

The hierarchy is continually suffering from the limitations of its sub-officers, and always trying to make them better links between the top of the hierarchy and the people on earth. This involves the art of communication.

In communication at the levels of thinking which can be expressed in words, teaching is distorted, simplified and deprived of its multi-dimensional scope. Communication on the physical plane can't be as subtle as on the mental plane, which in turn can't be as deep as on the soul level. If you communicate on a higher level, what you communicate is less concrete but more elevating to the soul.

Besides communication challenges, guidance is made difficult because the hierarchy does not order us to do things, they inspire us. First of all, most people don't believe that they are being guided, and some people would not like to do as they are instructed, as they have their own ideas. The work of the hierarchy is easier among people who wish to follow instructions, and are sensitive enough to pick them up.

Paradoxically the strong egos are the ones who can accomplish things on earth, but they are not sensitive enough to be directed by inspiration from within.

The highly attuned souls who hear the voice of inspiration often lack the power to carry it out in action. It is a rare being who is

both sensitive enough to receive guidance and strong enough to
carry it into action by battling with all the opposing forces in life.

Although Pir rarely spoke of it, on rare occasions he did mention
the existence of cosmic evil. It is in overcoming the dark forces, that the
light strengthens itself. There is a pair of opposites in all things; in each
there exists the spirit of the opposite. The two seeming opposites are a
necessary part of the higher plan of the One Being.

For me, the most fascinating of all Pir's stories was his story of
the black master. During a meditation when he was part of an esoteric
training group for young people, Vilayat found himself in the presence
of a group of masters. He noticed with surprise that one of them
appeared different with a dark appearance. They said to each other,
"What are you doing here?"

Soon his teacher joined them and said, "There always must be
a thirteenth, it is the law." After the session the teacher asked, "Do
you know who that was?" Vilayat answered, "No. Who was he" "That
was Trebitsch-Lincoln." "Who is he?" "Find out," replied the leader.
Vilayat discovered that he was a Hungarian who had been a member
of the British Parliament and had the dubious distinction of being
the only MP known to have hit another member while actually in
parliament.

Although there was no way Vilayat could have known it then,
Trebitsch-Lincoln was already well known to the intelligence services
throughout Europe. The story is told in great detail in a well-researched
book by Bernard Wasserstein entitled *The Secret Lives of Trebitsch-
Lincoln.*

Oddly enough, although he ended up working for the Nazis, he was
born Jewish in Hungary. He developed some extraordinary powers
as he was able to dupe even the French and British governments,
at least for a time. Despite a very checkered past, he managed to
get British citizenship and eventually get elected to Parliament. He
sold bogus German war plans to the French, offered his services as
a double agent to the British, was charged with forgery, and fled to
the US, where he wrote inflammatory anti-British articles, trying to
put the blame on England for causing the war. Eventually he was
jailed, but duped his jailers and managed to escape. Wasserstein

quotes him as saying, "I looked for another place where I could stir up trouble." In time he was persona non grata everywhere, including his native Hungary.

In 1927 he worked for three different warlords in China, then claimed to have converted to Buddhism probably to gain occult powers. He seemed to be sincere, but such powers may be employed equally for purposes of good or evil. Perhaps it was for this reason, he studied Tibetan practices and took a Tibetan name, one of his many aliases. He also spent time in a monastery in Ceylon, and next in 1931, was ordained as a monk in China, and promptly declared himself an abbot. As such, he collected disciples, all of whom he convinced to give their possessions to him. According to Wasserstein, he managed to damage all of them in the end.

Using his new identity he was able to get to San Francisco, where he studied Zen and even met Samuel Lewis, who considered him an ardent Buddhist, which in one sense he was. He practiced diligently, probably hoping to gain more power. However, there was no hiding from his past, which eventually caught up with him. In the end the only place where he could find refuge was the International Settlement in Shanghai. During the war, he helped both the Nazis and the Japanese by writing propaganda. He died in 1943.

It would seem that the story, and its sad ending, exemplifies not so much his mastery, but rather how Trebitsch-Lincoln was himself a pawn of dark forces, which used him, just as he had used others. It underlines the importance of what we choose to align ourselves with, but also points to the power and methods of the dark forces who were working through him.

Chapter 12
A SPIRITUAL GIANT

One reaches a stage when one is able to bring your consciousness down into the finest atom, to be able to expand your consciousness, until it encompasses the whole universe, and be able to reach into the depths of the void within yourself; to participate in all the joy of all the creatures, while at the same time remaining indifferent yourself, and yet at the same time know how to experience the ecstasy of the one who has freed himself from himself, and is conscious of the Divine Presence; know how to look at things without seeing through the eyes, and hear without hearing through the ears; how to be in the world and not of the world; how to meet with success and failure without being involved with it, at the same time straining yourself to achieve that which has to be achieved, and then hand the results over to God.
— PIR VILAYAT INAYAT KHAN

Pir Vilayat Khan was a spiritual giant and recognized as such by many. He had attained heights that few people alive could reach. Everything about him clearly marked him as extra-ordinary, his manner, his appearance and his speech It was his presence more than anything that made him so very special. It made him seem large, although he was not tall, but he so filled whatever space he was in, that it left one with that impression. When he was in a room all eyes naturally turned towards him. Cast in a movie he would always have been the central character.

By his accent and the words he used one immediately sensed that here was a cultivated person. His English and French were definitely those of a native speaker, but one would be hard put to say precisely from where. His face, and especially his nose, was finely chiseled, perhaps that of an aristocratic Afghan. His eyebrows very thick and black. His eyes brown and soft. His tact and refined manner all marked him as a man of education and sensitivity. His face was unusually expressive; at times his glance could be penetrating, at other times it showed deep understanding and compassion. Hearing him for the first time, one might come away bemused, confused, astounded, or uplifted, and on occasion all of these. At the least one would leave impressed, thinking here was a most unusual being.

For most of us, the respect or awe we felt would grow into abiding love. What was this attraction that he had? Once, speaking of the "Man of God," he seemed to be unconsciously describing himself:

> What is the power of the prophet, the man of God? When you come across a being who manifests sovereignty, great peace, authority, kingliness, it seems as if he is walking upon a rope with water on one side, spirit on the other, heaven on one side, earth on the other.
>
> You see, there is still the fragility of the human being in him, the imperfect self that is journeying towards perfection, and, at the same time, bearing the burden of numberless souls. It requires stretching your consciousness so high that on the one hand you can hear the voice of God and on the other hand the cry of human beings. This is a development of humanity that culminates in divinity.

One of his most attractive qualities was his smile. The child was still very much present in him, however it was not always easy to see, but one could glimpse it in his smile. It was a little boy's smile and was spontaneous and like everything about him, totally unaffected. Perhaps this was why he never tried to tell jokes. He had a wonderful sense of humor, but it would emerge entirely unplanned during his talks and seemed to come as a surprise to him. When he said something funny, his thick eyebrows would rise up in surprise and then we might see his shy, boyish smile.

His expressions on occasion could reflect what he wanted to express in a way that was at times quite dramatic. This was especially evident when he conducted a choir; it was then he became the embodiment of glorification or exaltation. When he was giving a blessing to children he became the epitome of loving kindness. There was never a hint of anything artificial; everything was totally genuine - always.

He spoke with great certainty and authority. Although he rarely asked for advice, he could be a good listener, especially to someone with expertise that he did not have. He was always willing to learn, but he suffered when forced to listen to fools. None the less he was always polite and could be very patient.

It certainly seems as if he taught from experience. He once said, "I never teach anything that I have not experienced myself." However, this did not stop him from speculating. At times he would apologize for indulging himself with such speculative questions as: "Does the programming take into account our decisions?" I wondered if one could actually get answers to these kind of speculations, especially since I found myself beginning to speculate about similar puzzles.

His knowledge on a many subjects was vast. On first hearing, one might guess him to be a scholar of comparative religion since he could speak with such authority about Zoroastrian angels, Valentinian Gnosticism, and any number of equally obscure subjects. In this one would be wrong. He was a born teacher, not a scholar. His knowledge was widespread rather than specialized in the subjects that interested him. His incisive mind could delve into everything from science to metaphysics but he was more intuitive than scholarly, and never used his knowledge to show off. There were also times when he could be quite wrong. Above all he loved to teach. Teaching also helped deepen his own understanding. His curiosity pushed him into areas where few others ventured, especially metaphysical and esoteric ones. His mind was brimming with possibilities and constantly generating new ideas, often original and sometimes profound.

Sometimes it seemed he was obsessed with hidden connections invisible to others. That was because he could see "The causes behind the causes" and grasp what he called "That which transpires behind that which appears" Seeing these hidden causes was one thing, but explaining them was a challenge. His insights were not just brilliant, but often way beyond what most minds could comprehend. This was an example of the way spirit veils itself, which makes it difficult if not impossible to explain to those who had not themselves been able to peer behind those veils.

In his father's absence, Vilayat had to map out his path for himself as there were no teachers available to help. The mystical journey by its nature is a solitary one, and each journey is unique. But Vilayat took this further. He was a lonely explorer, pushing to the edge of the known, and then pushing beyond, where there were no charts at all.

During his own retreats all he had to go on were the practices the yogis had given him, plus the dhikr. He did have his father's esoteric papers, but his father had not taught about retreats. In starting from scratch he had to break new ground and which was how in time he devised the Alchemical Retreat.

In order to help others to reach samadhi he had to figure out how he had first gotten into it himself. He assumed that what had worked for him would work for others, which was not always the case. Without any memories like his, we were handicapped. My previous experiences of samadhi had required months of sitting in a Buddhist ashram. There we were taught that in order to reach samadhi the mind had to become totally still which depended on much practice in building up one pointed concentration. This had clearly not been Pir's Vilayat's way. He hoped to guide us, but trying to listen to his words no matter how helpful, prevented me from stilling my mind sufficiently. Also the sessions we had did not allow enough time for me to accomplish this. Unless one had already "seen behind the curtain," what he said I found to be rather discouraging. Here is one of his explanations:

> When you get into the real samadhi, which is beyond the causal plane, you experience yourself as pure intelligence, pure spirit, or pure ecstasy and you have reached a point which is beyond becoming. This is the real samadhi which is not affected by what has been gained in the universe by its experience. It is beyond that. It's like seeing behind the curtain, the cause behind the cause and the archetypes behind all exemplars and finally the reality that is beyond all forms. It's like the highest level that consciousness can reach by extending beyond itself. One must have passed through that condition before one is able to maintain one's higher consciousness

while involving oneself in life.

This was what he called "Samadhi with open eyes," a phrase that we were to hear many times He seemed to imply that with determination it was a goal that we could certainly attain. However, the higher levels of samadhi proved beyond most people's reach, and I began to realize just how high this bar really was. Even after having such experiences, there was no evidence that he or anyone could maintain this awareness permanently in life. It was hard to say whether he unknowingly set unattainably high goals, or that he hoped he could help motivate us that way. I never heard him explain all the stages of samadhi systematically, but here is what I managed to glean from the many times he talked about them.

Starting with *savitarka*, the mind is stilled and thinking becomes rarefied, sitting becomes increasingly effortless. Next, in *nirvitarka*, thoughts cease, the senses fall away and one begins to merge with the object of concentration. In *savikara* and *nirvikara samadhi* all sensation and thoughts fall away, and the world is transfigured. There is no longer any awareness of a separate self but rather of a Universel Self. Mind has been replaced by Luminous intelligence. This is what Sri Aurobindo called *Illumined Mind* or *Overmind*, which he believed would only be reachable with further evolution. Finally there is *nirbija* or *asamprajnata samadhi*. In this one experiences the Clear Light which is also described as the "Pure Light of Bliss." No words can describe this, but Pir spoke of it as being a part of awakening.

Actually no words can adequately describe any of these states. Pir Vilayat would however, on occasion still try. He said that one became highly conscious without being conscious of anything in particular, and one was able to experience things from "God's point of view," which required losing one's identity. Once he explained it this way:

> Having experienced being carried beyond the consciousness of ourselves as separate beings, one can never be the same after that vision. The vision of the Self does not take anything away from the vision of oneness. Even back in our limited consciousness, one is forever transformed by that vision.

The Clear Light constitutes the underlying basis of mind and that experience is one that apparently only God Realized beings can reach. The mutual understanding they had was a clear sign of how similar these two paths could be. Pir could well be described as a pilgrim of the clear light. One of the reasons he so loved the high mountains was it was easier for him to help us reach those planes of diaphanous light and splendor.

He said that the Clear Light was not something that one could reach through conscious efforts, however, during advanced retreats he would still try to guide us through a series of steps to reach it. Starting with visualizing the aura, then leading up through radiant light and luminous landscapes that became ever finer, until one could hopefully enter the Clear Light itself. I wondered whether perhaps this was what he meant by going from gross mind to very subtle mind.

Light held a supremely important place in his life and teachings. What else could have impelled him to stare into the sun for an hour, even to the point of damaging his eyes. He explained the purpose of this was, "so that your eyes can look like the eyes of the sun." He often said, "Discover yourself as a being of light and then you can bring light wherever you go."

Once he sat longer than usual without moving a muscle. When he opened his eyes he said somewhat sheepishly that he had actually been asleep. It turned out that he had come back from a long trip, but this one was on a crowded plane along with some crying babies.

There was no question about his extraordinary attainments. He was a master who could delve deeply into hidden causes as well as the past and sometimes even predict coming events. For example, he had warned us several weeks before the Three Mile Island nuclear accident. However, what he foresaw was a worst case scenario with full meltdown In that case we were well prepared with stockpiled food and gasoline.

His most impressive ability, was to see deeply into one's soul. This was apparent when he was giving what he called his *darshans*. Here he might explain one's potentials that had not yet manifested, hidden blocks to progress, or even the purpose of one's life. He said it was the most difficult thing he did. There was a hidden cost to be paid for such abilities. Part of the price was that he felt overbearing egos and dishonesty in a way that was more painful than for most of us.

Probably he never completely fitted in anywhere, at least not on this plane. His memory of the realms of light and splendor was so compelling that naturally he longed to return to them. He also defied all categories. One could not say that he was a typical Sufi since there was no such thing. He disliked categories, perhaps that was why on occasion he would say, "I am not a Sufi," but in many respects he was. His dervish side was not always evident, but it showed in his deep longing for what the Sufis termed *The Beloved* and especially in his passion for truth and authenticity. He was totally devoted to his life's work, which was to spread his father's teachings.. This required him to involve himself in the world of people, to keep to schedules, and live according to the expectations of others. The extent to which he succeeded required both mastery and many sacrifices, since his deepest longing was to be free of all such cares.

Who is the dervish really? Was it the *madjub* with eyes of fire and a raucous voice who terrified and then awakening him? Without the constraints of himself, the madzub can become a flame that scorches. When his guide called out the name *Vilayat* he wondered who was that? In identifying with the all, who was left? Was that the dervish? Perhaps it was the hermit who emerged from the cave in Chamonix, but who was it sitting in the clear light under the tree in Bodh Gaya? And was that the same as the being walking majestically from his cave on the Mount of Olives, like a street lamp lighting up all in his path? There was also Majnun, lost in his love crying, "Who is Leila? I am Leila." The walls of the jail may be undermined by love. Without walls, where is the prisoner? And who is the being in ecstasy beyond joy, pulled ever further into the flames? Is he a sober dervish surrounded by a drunken world? Could such a soul ever be confined to a small stage?

Hazrat Inayat Khan described the dervish thus:

> His language becomes different. You cannot understand what his "no" means, or what his "yes" means. You cannot very well comprehend the meaning of his smiles, or of his tears. He may be sitting before you, but he is not there. He may be speaking with you, and yet communicating somewhere else. He may be among all and yet absent. You may think you hold him, but he is not there.

Once Pir attempted to explain it like this:

> The dervish is in the world, but not of the world. He sees all things happening, but he knows that they are not the way they look. The consciousness of the dervish is the consciousness of the One Being whose body is the Universe. The dervish experiences the emotion that becomes a flower. He is so intoxicated by love that he is incurable. Except for the Beloved, what is there to see? His soul is flying into the heavens and yet conscious of the reflection of the heavens on the earth. His very being is nostalgia, and yet he realizes this is the nostalgia of God, longing to see himself in another himself. He realizes that he is the one in whom God sees Himself, and that therefore he has to exist, although he would like to die.

The dervish is not bound by ordinary rules. He lives in a world where even the physical laws are changed in a way that make sense to him, but not to others. Here is the way that Pir explained it another time:

> There is a complete dedication to the reality of God; there is a sense of total annihilation, and at the same time an upliftment and a power, and an insight beyond anything one could describe. This is the fundamental truth of the dervish: he walks without feet, flies without wings, sees without eyes, and speaks in the silence. He is the instrument of the divine vision when he is no more there to see, and he is the instrument of divine love when he is no more there to love. His life is suspended beyond life and death — he is living a living death. Whatever affects him affects all beings, and whatever affects all beings affects him.

Naturally he breaks rules not made for free souls, like the crazy Zen masters laughing from their ink brush scrolls. They are laughing at the puppets who cannot see the strings. When asked how he had survived years the Cultural Revolution, one such master replied, "I took a long walk in the mountains." Pir could walk in the mountains, but not for long; his mission pulled him back. He found his freedom in the higher reaches of the spirit. He loved to take us with him on his high journeys. Lucky were the few who could climb so high. He explained:

> The man of God has wings of detachment and independence which frees him from self-imposed limitations whereby men enclose themselves in the cages of illusion.
> The hands and feet of the man of God are nailed on earth and free in the heavens. The hands and feet of most are free on earth and nailed in the heavens....The man of God transforms defeat into success, changes the face of the adversary into a friend, transforms sorrow into joy. For the man of God there is no darkness... for all is God. He dies a thousand deaths in the storms of the hearts of men so that he may resurrect them by his death...The non-manifest is for him the manifest. The one who does not see this will never understand the man of God.

It was no wonder he loved to fly. When he could no longer fly a Spitfire, then he could fly with his eagle. With the great bird perched on his wrist, he became an Afghan chief or Medieval Prince. He exalted when the jesses came off and the bird could fly free, high up with vistas growing steadily larger. Having tasted such freedom, who would return to that cramped world so far below? How many could share his vision? How frustrating to slowly walk once you have soared. His freedom came from realization and freedom from attachments, but also from surrender and mastery. As he said:

> Subservience to a person makes one a slave. Allegiance to the divine will makes one a king or queen. This is why Sufism is the tradition of the king in patched robes, which represents a blend of supreme will with unassuming selflessness: a remarkable combination of sovereignty with saintliness.
> The man of God is a king in a beggar's garb, a palace in ruins.

The dervish robe is the symbol of the destruction of the sense of personal autonomy. It is the combination of independent spirit with the renunciation of covetousness for possessions or personal advantage or position that makes for the ideal man.

When asked, "What is the difference for you between meditation and dreaming?" He answered, "In dreaming I know where I am going." Maybe so, but he often knew where he wanted to go in meditation, if not exactly the route he would use to get there, since he brought the music beforehand. Then again, he often began on one subject and ended up on another altogether. Sometimes he would start by switching his 'autopilot' on. For example, it would repeat well-worn phrases such as, " We need to perceive the implicit beneath the explicit." These words seemed to work like a mantra which helped him to raise his own consciousness. Soon enough inspiration would kick in and the direction might change. A talk, might become a meditation, or then again it could be the reverse or a combination of both.

We always looked forward to his mediations. As he entered the meditation hall all talking would cease and the atmosphere would subtly change. He mostly kept his eyes closed, but occasionally he would open them to stare at someone. Strangely many of us felt that he was speaking to each of us personally, and we sometimes discovered that he had answered our questions. Most often he did not try to plan ahead, and just trusted his inspiration to guide him. He knew the needs of the group would themselves determine the course he would take. When he was inspired, so were we.

He also understood that once he managed to elevate his own consciousness he could then help to lift us up. Perhaps at first only a few could follow him, but then he would descend and lift up a few more. Once up there with him, we were content to wait in those light filled, serene realms, patiently listening while he helped others ascend.

As he slowed down, his voice would grow deeper and the pauses would grow longer. Open eyes would all shut, thoughts grew less, and gradually cease. One was no longer aware of people or sounds in the room. As his inspiration flowed, he would captivate us. Gradually the magic theater would begin to unfold. One could never tell where the journey would be heading, but this was not of any concern. Since the flow was not planned, organization went by the wayside, digressions frequently intruded. It didn't matter. We were embarked on an epic adventure into higher levels of consciousness.

Books could do more than hint at the realms we might explore. It was as if he held the keys to unsuspected rooms, through doors that only he could open. Sometimes we might be carried along by his sheer brilliance, at other times one was barely aware of his words at all, then all thoughts and concerns would be left far behind.

In this magic theater his words became the soundtrack for an epic journey. We might travel with him into realms of sublime beauty, bathed with diaphanous light, or be filled with deep peace and serenity. One might even encounter the mystery of the Divine Presence and be filled with awe. Once it was over, one might find oneself walking on air, but strangely unable to remember a word he had said. Only looking back now, can I understand a little of how this magic could happen. At most he was the catalyst for a process in which we were all in together. He only seemed to be making it happen. Of course he knew this, and never claimed responsibility for any of it. In this way he was quite humble.

Clearly he could not just enter these exalted realms at will. At times the magic did not happen. As he said, "The higher stages in meditation cannot be reached just by one's own action, but solely by grace." Just as he was the catalyst for this grace, the group presence helped it to happen for him as well. Sometimes I felt as if I was the only one left out, and wondered how many others could follow him into all those rarefied realms. What was also clear was that I could not reach these on my own. After he departed, I feared that I would never reach such levels again. What I discovered however, was that my journey continued taking different forms. No doubt without such grand vistas, but progressing none the less.

Leading retreats he would sit immobile while the rest of us took our breaks and stretched. Once when someone asked him if it hurt to sit so long, he said in a casual way, "Oh yes, it's excruciating." However, one result was that he developed neuropathy and lost sensation in his lower legs. Walking became difficult for him, even with crutches. In the end he would warn us against following his example. Yet he liked to tell us of the dervish who could dance even though he could not walk. Not only could Pir control his emotions, but he had an unbelievable tolerance for pain. Once, just to test himself, he underwent a root canal operation without anesthetic.

He spoke with admiration, perhaps even a touch of envy, of the sadhus who could live high in the mountains without food and meditate in the snow. His attitude towards the body was something in need of control. One way he developed mastery was by setting himself challenges. The way he had learned German illustrates this. In the early days when he wanted to give a talk at a Sufi center in Germany, he was told by his uncle Ali Khan that he must do it in German. In order to do so, he wrote it out and then memorized the German translation. In a few years his German was good enough for him to dispense with a translator. He also learned Dutch by spending time in Holland, without bothering to take lessons. His first language was English but he said that he dreamed in French, which he actually had to learn when he was put in school in France not understanding a word at first.

The extraordinary strength of his will, which he had built up over years of self-discipline and austerities, created its own difficulties. He was aware of this and quoted his father, "Balance is the keynote of spiritual attainment. A virtue carried too far may become a sin." In a candid moment towards the end of his life he said, "It's very challenging to give up personal incentive, without just being passive and relying on levels of one's higher being to maybe take over" During another equally candid moment he explained how difficult it had been for him to surrender, in fact he doubted that he had fully managed it. This raised the question, when is surrender complete? Also, how much is it possible to merge one's will with the higher will? It seemed strange that this was something he was still struggling with in his last years. Perhaps the reason with his life long need for freedom.

Pir Vilayat said that in order to develop mastery, one must develop saintliness. "The master lives by will, whereas the saint lives by faith." Faith along with prayer, were two things he did not speak of very often. Speaking of the value of prayer, he described how the atmosphere in Cairo would change when everyone started to do their noon prayers.

Along with mastery he actually had his share of saintly qualities and regularly put the needs of others before his own. He was also blessed with an inordinate sensitivity, and felt the suffering of others intensely. At times he was on the verge of tears while telling us what had happened to his sister Noor and how he suffered nightmares reliving her death. For this he continued to blame himself. Yet there was nothing he could have done to protect her. The choice had been hers to make, not his. She had chosen to become a radio operator and, even when she was warned to leave, she chose to stay in Paris. Who would have thought that within such a soft, sensitive being was hidden such bravery, such steely strength?

Years after her death, he told us Noor had appeared to him. He said that her work was with prisoners, especially prisoners of conscience, and that she told him not to dwell on what had happened, that there was no way it could have been avoided. This seemed to have made little difference; the pain was still there. Not only had she been their "little mother" through the dark years after their father died, but she had long been the only one to whom he could fully open his heart. No words could express what she had meant to him and how deeply he felt her loss and suffered over the horrible way she had died.

Probably it was not just this loss that he was feeling; there had been so many other losses and betrayals. But there was no way he could talk about these without hurting others. Keeping all this to himself made the burden he carried that much heavier. One way to ease the pain was to transcend it in meditation.

He used Noor's story in another way. He often told us that we must try to forgive people who had hurt us. That meant trying to forgive the woman who had betrayed his sister for money and the guard who had beaten and killed her. In her case it seemed likely that he had never managed to do this fully.

A woman had once told him that after hearing him talk about the importance of forgiveness, she found that she was unable to forgive someone, and now blamed herself for her failure. As a result, Pir had a new concern: was he asking too much of people, and thus adding to their burdens?

In the many times he shared his pain over Noor's death with us, he helped us connect with our own pain and also making it easier for us to share our own with others. We suffered with him, and would gladly accept some of his burden; to the extent that we could do this, we were learning how to the carry pain of others, and most importantly, how to do this willingly. Perhaps this is the mark of real love.

His schooling at Oxford and especially his training as a British officer had molded him with the English reluctance to share deep feelings and the tendency to keep 'a stiff upper lip.' It had been the same for his father. Neither their cultures nor their roles in life made it easy to share many personal problems. Vilayat's psychological studies did not include Freud or Jung, nor had he ever had psychotherapy. However, he did recognize the spiritual dimensions of psychology. He had a great respect for Jung and frequently quoted one of his ideas: "If we do not face our shadow it will come to haunt us as our fate." He thought therapy was best left in the domain of those trained to do it, although he did say: "It becomes obvious that spiritual guides and psychologists would gain much by working together, since the factors they are dealing with interact and inter-mesh inextricably."

He emphasized the importance of examining one's conscience, especially at the start of a retreat, but perhaps he came too early to grasp just how useful the new techniques for self inquiry, including the power of group sharing, could be for what he was doing. The next generation of spiritual leaders, some whom began their training under him, have been introducing these into their own spiritual training. Many of these were first pioneered at Esalen, and further spread by techniques used in Werner Erhard's EST and A.H. Almaas' Diamond Heart work.

By nature Pir Vilayat was very private, which naturally was a challenge for such a public figure. He craved peace and quiet, but had to spend so much of his life talking to increasingly large audiences. He taught of the importance of keeping silent, and how we detract from our power by dissipating it in talk. This was just one of several reasons he sought solitude even at the cost of avoiding people that he was close to.

There was also the possibility that he unconsciously kept others at a distance as a protection against further hurt. He told us how he could feel his father's pain in reading his letters, which was often caused by those he trusted or depended on. Often there was no one that Pir could share his pain with himself, and their were few who could help him to carry the weight of all his burdens.

No doubt this is the challenge given to many great beings. Some of these burdens were unwittingly passed on to him by his father. He said, "What parents cannot complete, must often be completed by their children." Did he succeed in this I wondered? At the end he seemed to have had his doubts. He would write:

> The dervish experiences the displeasure of God in the intentions of men. He sees God handing himself into the hands of traitors in an act of love. He sees the whole drama of life in each droplet of the ocean of creation, and he sees it all working towards a great fulfillment. He would like to describe it and communicate it, but how can he do this? Who is going to understand the un-understandable? Who is going to understand the madness of one who has lost his mind in the realization of God? But such is the loneliness of the spiritual path itself.
>
> The dervish sees without eyes into the hearts of men — he sees their truth and their dishonesty, and he sees their intentions, their aspirations and their fears.

The years which he had spent reclaiming his patrimony took a toll which left deep wounds. Perhaps this also explained his need for respect. He suffered from a tendency to see threats to his position where there were none, and to push away leaders who only wanted to help and support him. He had a deep distrust of rigid or bureaucratic organizations and most especially rich spiritual organizations.

To understand Vilayat one must know the two archetypes he exemplified: the knight and the hermit. The knight dedicates himself to serving a higher cause by fighting the battles of life. The hermit's dedication is so profound that he is willing to give up all the pleasures of this world for the glorification of God and the attraction of the Spirit. For most of us, the two would be impossible to reconcile, but not for Pir. His solution, he explained, "To bring spirituality into the world will require us to instill something of the hermit into the way of the knight." One way that he did this was to spend as much time as he could leading meditations. To help maintain his attunement he needed to sleep and work in his own space, but he chose to keep on traveling constantly. One solution for this was to get a camper. He chose to follow the pattern his father had set by going to his students rather then letting them come to him. Inayat Khan regretted this and had planned to stay at home on his return from India, but that was not to be. It was his family that had suffered, as Vilayat's family would do in turn.

He had learned to live with an unusual number of contradictions just as we learned to live with his. He admitted to many faults, but rarely asked for advice. He could be very patient with the mistakes of others, but he was not really a patient person, which showed in how eager he was to move on after an event, no matter how lovely the location. He had great natural charm and was fascinating to listen to, but he rarely socialized. I could hardly imagine him at a cocktail party. He never engaged in small talk or used conversation to fill silences. He craved solitude, but was often lonely and needed companionship; yet he often pushed those who loved him away.

The key to understanding so much of what he did one must realize his need to be creating, constantly! This was the way his soul could best express itself. The creative artist in him was always seeking new openings, new possibilities. He became most fully himself when he was inspired and could see his latest creation take form. His God image was God the Creator. He sometimes thought of God as an artist who keeps on changing his mind. He said, "The central quality of God is creativity and we are the most godlike when we are creating and the universe can create through us."

The alchemical retreat format was a good example of this. Another fine inspiration was the Cosmic Celebration. In addition there was the Universel Temple in Suresnes and the Hope Project which initially provided milk and gradually grew into a school for poor Indian children giving them all important job training.

When inspiration came he might stay up late writing, or spend many hours designing a new kind of solar water heater for his cabin. These efforts required him to overcome limitations, both physical and conceptual. In the same way so much of what he wanted to express could not be said in words. Thus he was occasionally forced to create new ones, not bothered by how this made him harder to understand; it was all part of his creative process. The problem would then became ours, trying to divine his meaning. Often this seemed to require reading his mind.

His books provided the main outlet for his creativity, but he would lose interest as soon as one was finished. It was the process of creation itself that mattered, often at the expense of urgent matters or even the needs of his family. Immersed in his writing, he could shed his heavy burdens, at least for a while. Since new insights were constantly coming, in a few days he would change it again. Thus the books were never quite finished. Getting him to stop, became a challenge at which many tried but at which few succeeded. Turnover among his editors was consequently quite high. However, once a book or project was finished he would let go of it completely.

He was good at concealing the anger or impatience he often felt the same with showing his worries or doubts. He frequently said, "Mastery consists in never giving in to self-pity." These were examples of *Akhlak Allah*, as the Sufis call the manner of God. His anger when aroused could be fearsome, but it was under his control. He stressed the difference between anger and righteous indignation. He said, "One must become the Holy Warrior," a role that fitted him well. One could easily imagine him as a commander in the armies of Richard the Lionhearted or those of Saladin battling for the Holy City. He would write:

> Anger comes when truth has been violated. Pir-O-Murshid once said that the whole universe is a process so devised that truth may finally manifest. He said it is not enough that you say the truth; you must become the truth. That is what happened when Pilate asked Christ what is truth. He said, "I am the truth."
>
> Anger will trigger off the knight in one, it is an enormous power that redresses improprieties in order to affirm the divine order. It comes through particularly when facing injustice, when innocent people are being victimized. When one faces hypocrisy, when people are being manipulated. It culminates when the sacred has been violated; sacrilege one calls it. Maybe that is where our sense of outrage reaches its absolute limit. The Holy Warrior is prepared

to sacrifice, to be consumed by the power of the fire of righteousness, like the lamb on the altar, Agnus Dei. Part of the function of the knight is not just fighting evil, but giving succor to those who have been broken in life. That's also an expression of anger. One must find a way of reconciling the power of truth with the gentleness of compassion.

There were opposing sides to his character as well as some surprising hidden qualities. Occasionally the playful imp might emerge, which happened when he was dancing. Then he could throw aside his dignity and the fun-loving child would emerge. He took delight in telling us about jinns, these were not the powerful type that Aladdin summoned from his lamp, but unpredictable and imaginative forces who delighted in confounding one. I wondered was he speaking about beings he had met on the jinn planes? Did he realize how much he himself was a living example of just these same jinn qualities he so enjoyed telling us about? He could say the most outrageous things with a straight face. When this happened one was left wondering, "Was he serious?" He connected jinns with genius and creativity, no doubt not aware of just how much he was describing himself.

Because his own need for freedom was so great, he also extended it to others. As he disliked following instructions, whenever possible he avoided telling others what to do. At times difficult problems might be passed on for others to solve. Too many of these same problems were unfortunately also passed on when he died.

His duties may have chained him to earth, but when he could, he would head for the mountains and exult as his bird soared free into the endless clear skies. He told us of one eagle which had been locked in the dark for a year. After much thought, he felt he must try to help. This he knew could be fraught with difficulties. Fully grown eagles can be exceedingly dangerous. To rehabilitate it would require both patience and courage. Here is his account:

I retrieved an imperial eagle from a cage in a dark garage in a little town in Germany. With sharp talons and searing beak he attacked me as I entered the cage to place jesses on his legs. However, I will never forget the gratitude in his gaze as I took him out of the cage into the sunlight after a sequestration of over a year. I had gained his confidence. At first Majesty (the name I gave him) was even more afraid of losing me than I was of losing him. In time he learned that I would wait for him.

He was so overcome at the sight of the mountains at Chamonix, Switzerland, that he let himself be lifted by the breeze, soaring higher and higher above the clouds till the tiny speck had disappeared into the void. I shall never see him again, I thought; this time he has bid me adieu for good. What was my surprise when all of a sudden the speck reappeared and grew larger.... with a six-foot wingspan, in his mighty dive he knocked me over. This was his way of manifesting his joy at being home after his little escapade. Our friendship was sealed.

It is easy to see why he identified with Majesty. There had been so many dark periods in his life. In healing the eagle, he was healing part of himself. Perhaps this was why he never wanted me to film him at those times. He said it was too private. Sometimes Majesty was allowed to perch in the living room at Fazal Manzil, or in Vilayat's small study on the roof. There they both could look out on the Bois de Boulogne, where in good weather Pir would take him to fly.

Throughout the years Pir had a number of different birds, but he always hoped to raise an eagle from the time it was very little. His nephew Once, a gamekeeper discovered a nest with two eagle chicks. Only the stronger one could survive. When mother departed, Vilayat scaled the high tree and saved the smaller eagle. He named it Sultan.

Eagles and falcons are protected and no wild chicks can be sold in most countries. Thailand is an exception, where one could sometimes find babies for sale. For that reason he wanted to stop there on the way to India with Zia. Pir managed to find a baby falcon in a bird market. It was so small that he managed to sneak it through immigration in his pocket. However, the risk of a long bus trip to Dharamsala, where Zia was going to stay, was too great. Pir had to leave it with a student in Delhi. Perhaps it had bonded to him; it would not eat and lived just long enough to die in his hand when he returned, which was heartbreaking. He buried it next to the emperor Humayun's tomb. He had given it the name Temujin, the name of Genghis Khan. All his birds had regal names. This was fitting as so much of his life seemed to have been written for the big screen.

He would always bring a bird with him to the Alps camps. His yellow camper would be piled high with everything needed for the summer. Since he never took the time to pack carefully, things were loaded without plan. Space had to then be found for the eagle in its large cage as well. Size was a reason most falconers choose to fly kestrels, falcons or other smaller birds of prey, but not Vilayat.

Despite his failings, in all the years I knew him, I can think of nothing he said that struck me as egotistical, nor was there ever any sign of false humility. Publicly when he spoke about himself, it was generally to illustrate a point he was making. He somehow managed to do this while avoiding reference to his own high attainments, not an easy thing to do. It would have been so easy for him to exhibit a sense of superiority, but I never saw any sign of this. Nor was he ego-less. It was just that ego-centered statements were so painful for him. He was naturally gracious, and never belittled anyone. I also never heard him put anyone down. When he corrected someone, it was in such a way as to leave their pride intact. He always put great stress on this in his training for leaders.

He was so brilliant and his trove of knowledge so great, that at times it became a handicap. Once when he was asked just who was he writing for, he looked surprised, stopped and thought for a minute, then replied "Oxford dons." At age ten his father had said to him, "You will bring The Message to the intellectuals." Strangely he really believed that people came to hear him for his knowledge. It wasn't just his writing that was difficult to understand, it was the way he perceived the world which was beyond the average person's comprehension. For example, the way he frequently talked of "the implicate order hidden within the explicate," or saying how we must learn to use "subtle mind, rather than gross mind," yet he never managed to really explain what this meant.

Despite his vast knowledge, he was willing to learn, but mostly from those who had expertise. Sometimes what he knew would get in the way. Since as he said, "I remember Buddha" I suspect that was why he did not study his teachings more deeply. That made it hard to discuss the subject with him. His Buddhism did not seem to be the same as the ones in my Buddhist studies. Those lessons stressed the importance of mindfulness and awareness of the here and now. During meditations one had to observe sensations and what one was feeling. He rarely if ever mentioned such things. Staying and working with painful emotions that came up, especially in meditation, proved most useful for me. I suspect that accessing and working with repressed feelings was not easy for him, but certainly would have been a valuable addition to what he taught us. Luckily the next generation of teachers, whom he had helped train, were able to learn and teach techniques to do just these things.

Metaphysical speculation always had a fateful attraction for him. For example he could not resist puzzling over the classic Sufi conundrum over the difference between *wahdaniat*, *wahdat*, and *ahadiat*, i.e. how were unicity and unity different, and were they distinct from absolute oneness? However, he was also aware of the danger of falling into speculative traps.

On one occasion he recounted what it was like to go beyond all concepts. The event, described in his own distinctive style, happened when he was on retreat in the Alps late in the year, and not surprisingly there had been a violent storm. Here is his own account:

> After a stormy night in the mountains, sheltered precariously beneath the roof of a shepherd's shed, I observed the dark clouds and heard the thunderclaps gradually receding into the distance, swept away by a raging wind. As if in sympathetic resonance, my consciousness began to melt away, scattering into an infinite, edgeless Universe. Vanishing along with the storm were my concepts about the world, the Cosmos, my personal circumstances, unresolved problems, values, appropriate or inappropriate actions -- even my teachings about the Divine Qualities, the meaningfulness of life, egos, body, the psyche. Suddenly all these thoughts seemed so futile, worthless, and misleading! It was the consummate quantum leap; it brought vividly alive the last words spoken by my father, Hazrat Inayat Khan, on his deathbed, "When the unreality of life strikes my heart, its reality is revealed to me."
> All my life, I thought, I have prided myself on what I thought were valid theories about the Universe – unmasking the hoax of superstitions, dogmas, and conditioned responses to life. But instead of dismissing all these constructs, I realized that they had

acted as stepping-stones that led me to this ultimate breakthrough. Even though I now had no more use for them, they remained there for my use, like a ladder propped against a wall, while 'I' became immersed in the sublime, wordless state of unity beyond life, existence unveiled into eternity.

Despite such "ultimate breakthroughs," it is apparent how difficult it was for him or anyone to remain in that wordless state of unity beyond time. Did he hold this against himself? Even ascended masters choose a more functional state. Here was the essence of his dilemma, the everlasting tension between the transcendent and the immanent, that he was forever striving to reconcile for himself.

Hazrat Inayat Khan wrestled with the same dilemma. It seemed possible that Vilayat mentally compared himself with his father and felt that he was lacking. He was so young when his father died there was no way he could view him objectively. The image he retained was too perfect. Several times he told us, "He was always in God consciousness." Even if this was true, how could a young boy know this. His father's very greatness made it all too easy for all of us to idolize him as well. By the same token, one can see how difficult it must have been for Vilayat to have a father like Pir-o-Murshid and try to follow in his footsteps. This was of course a common problem for those tasked with following after great beings.

Under his favorite tree in Bodh Gaya

In Gangotri

Looking into the rising sun

The child within

Chapter 13
THE TASK OF THE GUIDE

Consider people's problems as your problems, while realizing that in fact there are no problems; thus you can help them see with the eyes of God. Do not load another person with your cares, do not expect what you cannot expect from another. Be all beings to all beings; a father and a friend and the son and the daughter and the servant and the king. Make your heart so wide that it is a treasure house in which all can find accommodation. It is not enough to love, one must understand. Love is the door to understanding. Know how to share your joy with all beings, penetrate into the hearts of all beings by your sympathy, not your inquisitiveness, and by the power of your love.
— PIR VILAYAT INAYAT KHAN, *THE GREAT JOURNEY*

Traveling the Sufi Path without a guide is like crossing the sea without a boat. The true meaning of the word *murshid* is guide. He is like the ferryman "who has surrendered to God and thus is an empty space, through which the wayfarer can reach the Beloved." In crossing the sea, the student is not able to judge his position, therefore the teacher needs to help him navigate. As Hazrat Inayat Khan said:

> I have not come to teach what you know not. I have come to deepen in you that wisdom which is yours already…I am the tide in the ocean of life, bearing all souls to the farther shore. One may attain the purpose of life without a personal guide, but to try to do so is to be like a ship traversing the ocean without a compass. To take initiation then means entrusting oneself in regard to spiritual matters to a spiritual guide.
>
> We must search, yet depending on our own efforts will not bring us to the goal. Without expending the effort one does not progress, yet our efforts alone can never bring us to the goal. If they could then there would be no place for faith and grace.

The journey has also been compared to crossing a desert; both a sea and a dessert are apt metaphors. Often one may feel lost in a desert where the oasis is just a mirage, or navigating an ocean where islands turn out to be so many clouds on the horizon. The journey has also been compared to climbing a mountain. A mountain guide naturally needs to know the route and have climbed it himself, and thus can help keep one from going astray. Pir Vilayat spoke of the need to have faith in the guide. He related how, on some perilous rock face, his guide would assure him, "You can do it." A mistake would be fatal. His guide knew just how hard he could be pushed, and of course how to first build up the necessary confidence in the young climber. In the end, Vilayat trusted him, took the risk and his faith and courage were both strengthened.

He also told the story of how there came a time when he had to climb without a guide to develop the self-confidence that he needed. By the same token there comes a time when we all must learn to climb without one. The teacher can serve as a ladder helping us to reach higher, but finally the ladder must be discarded lest it become a burden. Pir said, "In the end the teacher becomes the Friend." Here is one way he told us he had learned the teacher's role:

> When I was younger, I used to train falcons. You have a piece of meat on your glove, on your gauntlet, and you put the bird at a distance, and they fly to you. You increase the distance very gradually, so that they are tested in their faith that they will be all right if they come to your gauntlet, because birds are very timid. But you have to measure each day just exactly how much you increase the distance; if you increase the distance too much, they do not have the courage to fly that far and you are over stressing them.
>
> That is the art of the guru; he has to know how much he can test his pupil, and that depends upon the confidence the pupil has in him. It is a very fine art.

According to Hazrat Inayat Khan, the teacher is required to take a part in the process of melting the ego and then helping to transform it. He wrote:

Murshid's duty toward his mureed is as the work of the sun towards the plants. The sun gives its light for the plants to grow and flourish, to blossom and bring forth fruits and flowers. And in all these stages of the growth of the plant, there is a great part that the sun has to perform. So it is with the Murshid, who does not only give his experience in the spiritual path in words but by the life, the light, which silently helps the soul of the mureed to gradually unfold.

Pir sometimes spoke of seeing from the soul's perspective, to see without judgement and without projection. He said, "The teacher tells the student the truth of his own being. He tells him something which he already knows, but which his mind has forgotten." To do this it helped to know the purposes for which that soul had taken on form and what its potentials were. It is like giving the caterpillar a glimpse of the butterfly. Sensing a person's character and potential was essential in his role as master alchemist. He had to be able to see not just one's potentials, but what was blocking their realization or what caused the distortions. Pir Vilayat explained it this way:

> Our personality acts as a lens, distorting our divine inheritance, as in *The Picture of Dorian Gray*. For example, wrath facing injustice gets distorted as hatred, or mastery can become an ego trip, love into possessiveness, compassion can be distorted into indulgence, or cautious responsibility may become fear or timidity.

The marriage of the human with the divine is the great mystery that lies behind the great journey itself. How can the two come together? The single greatest obstacle for many students on the path, according to Pir is that they have damaged self-images or low self esteem. Perceiving themselves this way stands in the way of their soul's unfoldment. To overcome this, Pir hoped to help them discover an ideal and then develop the conviction that the ideal reflects what is already in them. In other words, the ideal is a mirror. What Pir wanted to do was open the student's mind. He needed to establish new patterns of perceiving. One way he did this was to raise us to the point where our minds were in harmony with his. He wrote, "The master lifts the pitch of one's soul, so that you may see what he sees, incorporate his being into your being, so that you may incorporate that which he incorporates of God into your being." He said, "Spiritual guidance is the art of making a being become what he is by helping him to see what he is rather than telling him what he should be." He often suggested that we try to see what qualities were fostered by the situations we were confronted with.

Pir Vilayat could see the possibilities latent in one's soul, and tried to help us see them for ourselves, and then begin to manifest them until they could achieve full expression. He explained:

> The ideal guru helps the person believe in himself with the power of his belief in that person. In fact the guru is really holding you high in his consciousness beyond your tendency to sink into your sense of limitation. He can give a tremendous uplift to you. To some extent, the guru takes on responsibility for you.
>
> The problem is with so many people the teacher must give what he can collectively and then work on the higher planes in his meditations. The guru is supposed to think of his students every day and always be in contact, especially in a crisis. He works with the pupil in his meditations.
>
> You mustn't think that it is just the soul of the murshid who uplifts the pupil. The soul of the pupil can uplift the murshid. There is a moment when the soul of the murshid has been deeply moved by what has happened to the pupil and then you know that you are in it together, in this great search for divine perfection.
>
> The link between the pupil and the murshid is so deep, the deepest thing that there is. And then there is the ecstasy that is communicated from one being to another, the pupil can sometimes inspire the teacher and it is natural that it works both ways.

The alchemical marriage comes from realizing both our human and divine inheritances. One needs to accept that the ideal is possible and then develop the courage to make it a living reality. In many ways Pir showed it was indeed possible to achieve this. One of his favorite sayings was, "Dare you have the courage to be who you really are?"

When he was inspired Pir could be a master of words, but his most important work was not done in words. What he really hoped for was to help give us the experience. No matter that his words were often abstruse or theoretical, they served his purpose. For this we had to be in his presence; recordings could help, but mostly they served just as a reminder. It was often hard to remember more than a sentence or two of what he said; it didn't matter. The effect was lasting, whether we knew it or not we were being transformed. The nature of this transformation would only became clear many years later.

Part of his mission was to help angelic souls cope with some of the difficulties of incarnation. He hoped that the Abode could serve as a refuge for people like this. One way he could do this was by putting us in touch with the angelic aspects of our being and thus helping us to remember the angelic inheritance which we all had, but had lost touch with. For this he often used music. The piece which he used for this had actually helped him to discover what he called "the hidden child within." It was the *Pie Jesu* from Andrew Webber's Requiem sung by a boy with a pure angelic voice. This inspiration would become one of his most effective healing techniques. People often cried when we played it during his sessions.

Pir also knew that there are times when "You have to see yourself in another yourself in order to know yourself." He himself was so multifaceted, and exhibited so many fine qualities, that he could serve as a role model without even realizing it. We could not help but be inspired by his modesty, generosity, compassion and nobility. By serving as an example he helped us gradually build an ideal which would then inspire us. He said we must learn to have compassion for our human weaknesses and clearly showed it by his understanding of human limitations. He also knew the danger that one's ideal could be turned into a cross and cause one to blame oneself for not being able to live up to that ideal.

He hoped to help us see from the soul's perspective instead of the ego's. The purpose of the soul was different from that of the ego. Whereas the ego sought admiration, recognition, and pleasure, the soul sought wisdom, and to develop divine qualities so that it could progress spiritually. Pir could see the potentials latent in one's soul and wanted to help us see these as well. The wazifas he selected for us were chosen to develop qualities he could see were latent and needed encouragement.

One way he described this was "To make God a reality by awakening the God within." This meant helping us find the teacher within ourselves and then using the wisdom we had in each of us, which he called part of "our divine inheritance." He liked to explain this in terms of restoring old recordings of Caruso:

> To know what one's defects are one needs to recognize one's qualities and earmark the distortions of those qualities in one's personality. If one is not extremely scrupulous about being honest to oneself, one tends to fail to recognize this distortion and firmly believes that one is acting under the higher impulse. This distortion can be redressed by confronting it with its archetype, just like light distorted by a concave lens can be reconstituted to its original pattern by a convex lens.
>
> Caruso's voice which was distorted by the recording machines could be restored to its original beauty just as if we were able to reverse the arrow of time. Even so, our divine nature, suffering from defilement like a distorted exemplar of a perfect archetype, can be reinstated to its pristine glory.

Pir often said, "If you could only sit here and see how beautiful you look." His aim was to help us to perceive ourselves this way and hopefully begin to see with his eyes and feel some of what he felt. He tried various ways to help us see our unrealized potentials, latent qualities which he could sense but of which we were unaware. Purification practices, meditation, and self-observation were part of it. He himself could see people's potentials using his extraordinary intuition, which was what he called his "X-ray vision."

He wanted to help us develop our own intuition. It was not easy to teach this, as there were no rules to go by. To develop intuition Pir emphasized the importance of learning to be truthful, being truthful to oneself was the hardest part. One also had to learn not to rely on one's rational thinking, which proved difficult indeed. When what seemed to be intuition proved wrong, rather than doubting it, we should use this as a way to improve it. The process required developing the habit of watchfulness, "to check and recollect how one felt every time one had a hunch that was confirmed," and "to suspend thought each time an intuition emerges." Then must trust and act on it.

It was important to learn how to be receptive. While spotting submarines, he learned he had to use his peripheral vision. Pir said we need to use "the peripheral vision of our mind." " We counter intuition with our thinking. Therefore we must question the validity of our thoughts and realize that things are not the way we think them to be, even if this meant going against common sense." To intuit the condition of another, he taught that we must learn to experience their condition within ourselves. In doing this he warned against using visual and other clues, although these were important, depending on such clues could mislead one. In this case it would be better to try to sense a person's 'atmosphere,' rather than their appearance or expressions.

Based on the same principle Pir preferred not to tell us the meaning of the wazifas which could be limiting; instead he wished us to get into the feeling of it. As he explained, "The meaning detracts from experiencing the reality of the wazifa which is an emotional attunement and then the wazifa will really work."

As one learns to better hear the 'still small voice,' it becomes more dependable. Intuition is based upon a totally different dimension which he said depends on trust rather than skepticism or beliefs that have been instilled in us. He said that "it is based upon a kind of precognitive knowledge beyond the mind," which he calls the knowledge of the soul. It depends on what he called "a network of signals" that does not go through the regular channels. When we ask for guidance he said, "it really amounts to calling on your intuition." One of the reasons why renunciation and surrender is so important is that "by giving up our will something deeper that is a self organizing faculty can start coming through."

All of this was part of the process of learning to think, "luminous thoughts" and training in grasping "the implicit beneath the explicit. In fact we were learning a new way of using the mind, which in time would take us beyond what was usually even thought of as thinking. Sri Aurobindo believed that in both our individual and racial evolution, we were destined to graduate from ordinary mind into what he called 'Higher Mind' and 'Illumined Mind.' These involved totally different ways of thinking and would he hoped be developed over time.

At the end of a retreat, when the level of presence was high, Pir would sometimes put himself in a special altered state and give *darshan*. In this state he was able to allow a higher or kind of super-consciousness to take over. This was not the same as channeling as done by psychics or mediums. He was aware of what he was saying, although often surprised by what came forth. We would sit before him, one at a time, and he might reveal the deeper purpose of one's life, or the unknown blocks that one needed to overcome.

It was clear that Pir was doing the kind of spiritual deed that Joseph Campbell described as a form of the hero's journey, in which the hero learns the hidden aspects of events or people's lives and then comes back with a message. On occasion it might involve what he called glimpsing the "Higher Plan," when he could speak of events to come .

There came a time when he announced that he would no longer be giving these darshans. He said it was one of the most difficult things for him to do. He also knew just how fallible he could be. This was something we always eagerly anticipated and sorely missed its absence when he stopped doing it.

To take on responsibilities for others was a heavy responsibility in itself. He had a willingness to acknowledge his own limitations which showed an honesty and humility rare among famous teachers:

> Living up to the need of the guru image in people forces me, and indeed all those in a leadership position, into a role in which one runs the danger of neglecting to confront one's own defects and weaknesses or inadequacies. Because of a pupil's awe in the face of the aura of the guru, it is sometimes difficult to unmask the justifying resorted to by a person looked upon as an example....This is a typical guru syndrome which we are witnessing in our time: masking contradictions, instead of recognizing their incongruity and correcting them. At some point the Guru must fall from his pedestal so that we can find the guru within.

This was both a difficult challenge for him, and for us as well. Unconsciously we all wanted him to be perfect since we hoped that he could fulfill the role of the wise all knowing teacher. Thus one of the risks he took giving darshans was that it gave the impression that he was all knowing, although he knew he was not.

He understood the student's tendency to project their own needs unto him. This was one of the reasons he stopped giving them. He was quite aware of his own limitations, and the potential dangers that could result. He said that it would require a being like Al Hallaj to say, "The light of the divine awareness has risen in my heart, like the sun over the horizon, and it will never set." It was for this reason that he helped make archetypical figures such as the Buddha, Mohammed, Christ, Mary, or Kuan Yin come alive for us, and then urged us to invoke them for ourselves.

Rather than relying on his darshans for guidance, Pir Vilayat suggested that we meditate on the being of a master. Unlike traditional gurus, who tell their students to meditate on the guru himself, he would never suggest using himself this way but he often suggested using Hazrat Inayat Khan. Here is how he described the process:

> Hazrat Inayat Khan gave instructions to his mureeds to meditate on his presence just before going to sleep. .... He said there are several stages in this union; the first one is *tasawuri murshid*, which is representing to yourself a picture of the face of the master which incorporates his being. The picture can become a limitation unless it is understood as a stepping stone, so this is only the first stage
> We have to go beyond the picture into Hazrat Inayat Khan as he is now, at present. What we encounter then is far beyond anything in the photographs. It is far beyond anything that we could ever imagine with our wildest imaginations; the grandeur, the greatness, the light, the power, the atmosphere, the joy, the ecstasy, the love, and the magic — it is beyond description. Here we have gone from *tasawuri* Murshid to *tawajeh*, which means going beyond the picture into the qualities of the master.

The ideal teacher would be empty, a clear channel to transmit the divine presence and equally able to manifest unconditional love, wisdom, or majesty. The murshid strives to open the mureed's heart by being a channel for 'ishq, unconditional impersonal love. It is fitting that the word inayat means loving kindness, while the name Vilayat comes from word wali, meaning the friend or the protector.

This was the ideal, what is called insan-al-kamal, the perfected being. But in real life of course, no teacher could be this perfect. He said,

> I can't say the pupil is limited by the personality of the teacher, because the teacher is supposed to be concentrating on his teacher, so the whole line of the teachers is supposed to come through if the teacher is empty enough himself.
>
> That is the reason why Rumi said the real murshid is the one who kills the idol that people make of him. On the other hand the personal contact with a being who communicates something beyond himself is a key to spiritual unfoldment, much more important than all the instructions or meditations that one could possibly give. The teacher gives as much as he can collectively, and then works on the higher planes in his meditations. That means thinking of his pupils every day.

Pir illustrated this with a story he told about one of his teachers who it appears may have been some kind of sadhu or dervish but he never told us anything more about him:

> I had a guru; I met him in the train station in New Delhi. There was a man who reminded me of Murshid, he was illuminated. I saw him going up the steps to the first class waiting room. I went and bought something to offer him and in my bad Hindustani I presented it to him and he answered me in perfect English. I said I already have a teacher, but he answered "It doesn't matter, if you want we can just sit and meditate a little." In the end we used to sit meditating for hours. He didn't really teach me, it was just a kind of attunement. At one point a policeman came and asked for our papers. He didn't have any papers of course, so the policeman said, "What is your name?" He answered "Bhagavan." Bhagavan means God. The policeman didn't understand at first but the funny thing is in the end he became his disciple.

Pir called the dhikr "The ultimate practice." It was the most effective way the Sufis had to work on the nafs or lower self. His dhikrs could be awesome. Sometimes it seemed like he was opening the portals for Al-Hallaj, Ibn Arabi, or Inayat Khan to come through him. The words might be the same: 'La illaha illa'llah hu', but the power and presence coming through were certainly not just his own. When he led them, which was not often, we never knew what to expect; perhaps it would be "The Dhikr of the Broken Heart" or "The Dhikr of Divine Power" or it might be "The Dhikr of the Crown of Glory" or "The Dhikr of Divine Majesty." Their names alone give some sense of how powerful and majestic they could be.

Over the years Pir had done a great deal of dhikr himself and despite all his attainments, continued to do it on his own retreats.

> The dhikr confers on you a very great strength that one could never find in oneself. There is absolutely no comparison between the greatness of this reality and the insignificance of what humans attain or achieve.
> The beauty of the dhikr is that it attacks the foundation of one's assumption of being an individual person. As our concept of the self as a discrete entity is destroyed, God is dying and resurrecting in each of us. The whole aim is to bring the divine glory, power, majesty, splendor, and light as well as purity and truth down into your being.
> If you let yourself be carried into the mystery of divine love, it is beyond the majesty of the heavens.

Pir Vilayat had such vivid memories and such a deep connection with his father that he could bring him alive for us. This was part of a process ending up with *fana fi sheikh*, where on entered the consciousness of the teacher. This was an important step in linking with the great masters and the prophets. That was one reason that Pir tried to make them real for us. Equally important was developing a high enough attunement so as to reach these great beings. The higher one's attunement the higher the beings one can reach. The next step would be to enter into the consciousness of the prophet or avatar, which is called *fana fi rasul*. It was through him one finally merges one's consciousness with the One Being, *fana fi'llah*. This was part of forging the mystical chain linking us to our *silsilla* and the great beings that were part of our lineage. Taking initiation was the first step in linking up with a master.

It was often misunderstood. As Pir explained:

> Initiation is a kind of covenant. In fact bayat means a covenant, and in a covenant there is always the words "I will." It is always like a promise of course. The question that is asked is: 'Will you consider that which is given to you as a sacred trust. Will you give your allegiance to the Message of Unity.' It's what is called fealty, giving you loyalty to the Government of The World is what it really amounts to.
>
> Bayat is a pledge. Having given one's confidence to the teacher, one pledges to fare into untrodden lands, and the teacher gives his confidence to one. The murshid is the link between the mureed and his *tariqa*, the chain of teachers that went before. Initiation corresponds to the lifting of the veil of ignorance. Further awakening is always preceded by a purification which may assume the form of a test or trial. One may be forced to make a choice, whether one's heart is on earth or in heaven. One's life may break down and familiar worlds may crumble....The initiation takes place on the completion of the test when the lesson has been learned. It is always a victory over limitation and ignorance. The end is a celebration.
>
> A master will generally link the one who asks him for guidance by the same type of pledge that he himself has solemnly taken, which includes the karmic responsibility for the growth of the initiate whom he of course does not solely carry upon his own shoulders, but shares with the hierarchy. This act may precipitate a transformation in the initiate, if its timing corresponds to a real threshold that the initiate is passing through in the natural unfoldment of the path before him. In these circumstances the initiation acts as a catalyst, accelerating slow progress. One's progress along the path proceeds through certain stages, stations, and states.
>
> Depending on the nature and grade of initiation, different strata of beings may be called upon. When initiation is for service rather than personal progress, it is ordination, passing from the aegis of Elijah to that of Melchizedek. When it involves the teaching of the mysteries, it passes into the realm of Enoch or Hermes. When it involves militant social action it is under the jurisdiction of the Archangel Michael; healing that of Raphael; and when it is prophetic it is in the realm of the Archangel Gabriel. Thus a particular initiation may affect one's multidimensional

aspects connected with a cosmic principle, such as planetary, lunar, solar, galactic, and even universal initiation.

Some people took initiation without understanding the nature of the mystical link it created. Students would sometimes leave and take other teachers without even having the courtesy of letting him know. The result was that Pir was left holding what he once called " dead lines."

I think Pir Vilayat was more a healer of souls and minds than of bodies. Perhaps the way he developed mastery over his own body contributed to this. He seemed impervious to pain. His father had believed that we should try to welcome pain as a teacher. However Pir was not much given to analyzing painful sensations or feelings. It also seemed to me that he may have doubted his own ability to heal. When he taught healing he seemed to stay close to what his father had taught, namely the use of magnetism, light, and the Holy Spirit, using the mantras *Ya Shafi* and *Ya Khafi*.

Pir Vilayat understood that there were potential dangers and stressed these in his instructions to healers. He cautioned them about using the wrong energy which might exacerbate illnesses such as cancer.

He was wary of the risk of giving people overly high expectations. He stressed the importance of love and empathy in healing. He said, "In order to heal, you must be willing to take on the suffering of the person you are healing," and also, "The first principle in healing is joy." This was something he excelled in. Another way was through laughter. His humor came spontaneously without effort. But music remained his most effective remedy, especially that of Bach. His delight dancing to the Ressurexit was infectious.

Some of the leaders he trained in healing became fine healing teachers in their own right. Himayat Inayati relished telling us how when Pir appointed him to head the Sufi Healing Order, he asked him what it would take for him to become a healer. Pir responded, "In order to heal you must be in a state of pristine glory." Just what this entailed he did not say. Himayat had no idea either, but he was willing to try and find out. Perhaps he succeeded; if nothing else it made for a great story. In the end, pristine or not, he took on the challenge He greatly expanded its reach and went on to create the Raphaelite School of Healing. Thus an expanding web of healing circles were created. They played an important role in invoking angelic help and healing not just people but our planet as well.

One of the murshid's tasks was to teach the mureeds *adab*: such things as respect, courtesy, humility, obedience, and the importance of selfless service in general. Pir Vilayat was not one to lecture his students on these subjects. His way was to teach by his own example. He disliked using the word "should," and in this he followed his father's example.

At times one had to be able to intuit his meaning and to be fully attentive to his wishes, which were often implied and said without words. He could be very subtle. Once he asked me to do something for him. I made the mistake of asking if it could wait, so that I could hear his upcoming talk. The way he said, "Oh yes, there is no hurry at all," drove the point home as no reprimand could ever do. On another occasion he asked a mureed, "Can you see that from the other person's point of view?" The student thought briefly and then answered, "Yes, I think I can." Pir responded, "Oh really. I never can."

Among aspiring Sufis one sometimes hears such things as, "The murshid has such strong baraka" but *baraka* is not something one has that can be given. It is received by grace, and the teacher can serve as a conduit, no more. He described it thus, "Baraka is much more than a blessing. It is part of the central mystery; the dervish doorway that energies can move through." We were so very lucky to have a teacher that could help us in this way.

The heart of the Sufi path is the mystical connection to the teacher and one's *tariqa*. This is the reason that a teacher is required. In some cases the teacher may even have passed on. This is uncommon, but still possible. But what if one does not have a teacher?

How can one find the right teacher, and how does one judge? In many traditions a search is required which entails passing tests. If this is the case, the search is part of the path itself, and the tests are a measure of commitment. From a deeper perspective, the process begins on the inner planes when we are ready. It only appears that the student succeeds in finding the teacher; it is equally true that the teacher finds the student. However, this is hard to grasp until one understands the underlying process of which we are all a part. The teacher has a hand in molding the student, but there is much truth in the saying, 'The student creates the teacher.'

The extent to which the teacher has mastered his or her ego and allows him to reflect back the student's ego and help free him. Thus the teacher appears differently to each of us. For some mureeds, their deepest connection was with Hazrat Inayat Khan. In this case their connection to him was through Pir Vilayat, but it was Murshid who would be the boatman guiding their boat to the other shore whether they knew it or not.

Through devotion and his example, the teacher can inspire devotion and willingness to surrender in us. What makes surrender so difficult is that it undermines the ego. It threatens our freedom and our sense of self. In fact, one act of surrender is not sufficient; rather, we have to keep on surrendering. We are surrendering to God, but God is not reasonable. The murshid knows this and may make unreasonable demands as tests. For a test to be real, there must always be the possibility of failing it. As we progress, the tests get stiffer. The greater the being, the greater the test.

The sense of being known, being deeply understood, perhaps for the first time in one's life, helps explain the mysterious attraction Pir had for us. He could reach us on the soul level. Most of us didn't understand what this was, let alone know that such a thing was possible. He explained the process this way:

> You communicate with the inner beings of people, and they feel it. Sympathy will of course establish a connection, but the fact of actually communicating with the souls of people, that's the greatest link there is. It will establish a far deeper connection. Therefore it's not good enough to love, one has to also understand. Love is the door to understanding.

When giving darshans he could see the mistakes we were making and sometimes the dangers ahead. He knew that when he gave warnings these were all too often ignored. He also knew that mistakes were part of the process of transforming the *nafs*, the Sufi term for the ego, and that learning from one's mistakes was an integral part of the process. He sometimes gave hints. Our challenge was to pick up and act on them. This entailed a degree of trust, as well as willingness to learn and surrender.

There was a fine line between giving advice and making choices for people. He knew the risks of interfering. Then there was the question of how much guidance to give. He did not want students to become dependent on him, but to develop their own knowing. Here is what he wrote: "The guru instead of helping you will stand in your way, if he allows you to become dependent on him. Unless he is empty of himself, he will root you still deeper in the core of your limitations."

A spiritual relationship was a new experience for us that created its own challenges. The problem was that we were used to personal relationships. The relationship with the teacher ideally could entail a melting of the heart and a merging. This was difficult and could result in much heartbreak. In the process, one was forced to leave behind so many preconceptions, ways of thinking and behaving. How was it possible to feel so much love without a personal relationship with the teacher? Could an intimate relationship be impersonal? The teacher had to exercise care to avoid potential entanglements with students that could be harmful to both of them. Even knowing where the fine red line lay was a challenging task. The student, without understanding this, was often left confused or at times hurt. This is one reason teachers often keep a degree of remoteness; just how much varies with the individuals. This was just one of the many things that the Pir could not explain.

The trauma of losing all those he loved so dearly had never been completely healed for Vilayat. Although he had healed his depression, there was still much deep pain. One could understand why he might protect himself by not allowing himself to become vulnerable again. This took its toll and was why he said, "Don't ask me questions about romantic relationships. I haven't been able to work those out myself."

There was also the nature of his work which forced him to shield himself. To maintain his fine sensitivity he had learned how to protect it. He needed to be shielded from the importuning of students who wanted to greet or question him. I never heard him actually request it, but one of us always walked beside him to act as a shield. He needed to maintain his concentration before a session. Afterwards it was difficult for him to even speak. Walking with him then, you could feel some of the vast consciousness that he was holding.

His manner almost always discouraged personal conversations, but there was a price we paid for this. I was to discover that one of the unfortunate results of the distance he kept was that both of us carried misconceptions which could have been cleared up with just one heart to heart talk. I realized that in his self-imposed isolation he lacked feedback that he needed. I wonder how much he realized this. I had assumed that with his ability to reach one on the soul level and with his fine intuition he could also know anything he needed to about me. I was wrong. Nor did he understand the depth of my love for him, something I only discovered myself after he was gone. By the same token, he did not understand how much he had helped so many of us and how much we had all loved him. I had thought that I was long past grieving for him, but writing of it now fifteen years after his passing, brings back the void that he left, and I guess that will always be with me; others tell me the same.

Sunrise meditation

Chapter 14
THE PARTING OF THE WAYS

Trust yourself as a glass into the hands of all people, and at the same time hold the secret of all beings in your heart as a sacred trust. Know how to free another person by involving yourself with that person and free yourself by involving yourself in life. Do not be disappointed if they do not turn out to be what you expected.
— PIR VILAYAT INAYAT KHAN, *THE GREAT JOURNEY*

There is a contradiction in the concept of a Sufi order. Since the dervish cannot be limited by rules or even simple definitions, how can he be part of an organization that restricts his freedom? Hazrat Inayat Khan himself was not one to create rules or enforce discipline. One result was that he suffered from oversized egos and conflicts within the Sufi Movement. This was part of the reason he moved to France and quite possibly why he left for India, after leaders of his organization attempted to control him.

Traditionally Sufis belong to lineages, but they do not have formal organizations, in the way they have here in the West. In India Suffism was widespread, but to spread his message in the West Pir-o-Murshid needed the help of others and for this an organization was required. However, on his death there was no one with both the spiritual attainment and charisma to head it. Clearly he was irreplaceable. Not only was there no one who could take his place, but he left no instructions on how to carry on. Without him a number of the organizers soon left. With no one at the helm, the ship almost foundered. His brothers and cousin took over, but it could never be the same. The American organization had never been strong and in time Meher Baba took it over and made it into something else he called Sufism Reoriented.

On his death the senior membership of the Sufi Movement could not agree over the choice of a successor. Murshida Martin, his first student, had long been the head of the American branch of the Movement. She came to Europe expecting to be appointed as his successor, but the European leaders would not accept her. No woman had ever headed any Sufi order, let alone one born Jewish. To make matters worse, her manner turned everyone against her. For example, she chose to address them as "my mureeds," whereas Pir-o-Murshid had always said, "Beloved Ones of God."

Tentatively it was decided to appoint Maheboob, the oldest of Murshid's brothers as 'Representative General'. However, this choice caused deep disagreements within the organization itself, which split into two opposing camps. Maheboob himself had been trained as a musician, not as a teacher. He said that he could not possibly fulfill his older brother's role nor did he have the initiation for this role. However, after some time the decision was made to appoint him as Shaikh-ul-Mashaikh (Sheikh of Sheiks) rather than Pir. On his death in 1948 he was succeeded by Ali Khan, Murshid's cousin, who was known for his abilities as a healer and good voice. Finally, the younger brother Musharaff, took over the leadership in 1956. During this time, Vilayat had continued his lecturing and classes independent of the headquarters, but still under the auspices of the Sufi Movement.

Some of the ongoing issues that divided the Movement had become deeply entrenched and were difficult to heal. These were not just personal differences. There were financial disputes and divisive issues of ownership of property as well as the contentious issue of Murshid's succession. One of the groups which included Pir Vilayat and members of the Geneva headquarters had different conceptions of what the mission of the organization should be. The brothers, who now lived in Holland, in their reverence for Murshid wished to do things just as he had done. Vilayat shared the same reverence, but besides this, he was committed to change and to the emerging new consciousness, which Murshid had actually pioneered, but which was slow in emerging in Europe where old traditions was very strong.

Shortly after the death of Ali Khan, Vilayat received the formal recognition as a Pir in Ajmer by two Chishti Sheikhs: Diwan Sayyid Saulat Husayn and Sayyid Faruq Husayn. In his own mind, Pir Vilayat always considered this of lesser importance than his father's wish that he should become his successor. One indication of this was that during the final ceremony before his departure, Inayat Khan had asked Vilayat's mother make a yellow robe for him. Another thing was that when Fazl Mai Egeling had died at the end of 1939, she left her money in a Dutch trust specifying Vilayat as the beneficiary in his capacity as "Leader of the Sufi Movement," which was very much in accord with sentiments prevailing throughout the organization at the time. As Mahmood Khan, the son of Maheboob Khan, recalls "Among all Sufi members it always had been idealistically assumed that Vilayat in time would succeed Murshid." At one time during a discussion for the successor, Hidayat's son Fazal, who in time himself would be chosen for the role, is reported to have said, "Vilayat will outshine all of us."

In 1957 Pir Vilayat took over leadership of the Sufi Order, which was the esoteric branch of the organization, but which for practical purposes became independent of the Sufi Movement. His other uncle, Musharaff, who then headed the Sufi Movement, died the next year, but by then the split had become too wide to be healed. One of the differences was that the leader of the Sufi Movement after Murshid died, had always been decided by committee and the leadership wanted it kept this way. Pir Vilayat insisted on the right to choose his own successor. The Movement's silsilla included Hazrat Inayat Khan's brothers and Ali Khan, whereas the Sufi Order, headed by Pir Vilayat did not. These seemingly small issues had some very important implications.

The disputes came to a head, and to Vilayat's deep disappointment, the money set aside to build the Universel in Suresnes was used to build one in Holland instead. The location chosen by the beach in Katwijk was one that Murshid had felt to be special, but he had been clear that he wanted the Universel Temple to be built in Suresnes. The choice of Katwijk reflected the ongoing dispute between the leadership in Holland and at Suresnes. It was opposed by a number of the leaders and widened the growing split between the two groups within the Movement until it precipitated the final separation.

The Sufi Movement leadership tended to criticize Vilayat to their students. Despite this he felt he could not speak out against members of his family. Thus, no explanations for the growing disagreements were ever made public and the reasons for the split remains untold to this day. The result, all too common among many organizations, been an ongoing pattern of silence and rumor.

In February of 1968 Pir Vilayat registered the Sufi Order in London as a separate organization, a revival of the original Sufi Order which Inayat Khan had started there. Later in that year, Hidayat's son Fazal was appointed to be the head of the Sufi Movement, but the direction he took it in was not acceptable to the leadership. In 1982 he decided to step down, and in 1985 he started his own organization, which he called The Sufi Way.

Pir Vilayat had to build the Sufi Order from the ground up. With little organization or money, the work went slowly. It would seem that the pull of his destiny might slow him, but it could not be stopped. Inayat Khan had received much help from the Theosophical Society. Many members were waiting for a great master from the East. Annie Besant, its leader, at first believed that Inayat might be the one they had been waiting for. The Society gave him important support in arranging facilities for his talks. More and more members left to become his students. A number were wealthy and gave him needed support. Pir Vilayat did not have any such advantages; however he was a magnetic speaker and attracted larger audiences than anyone since his father. He gave talks in Germany, Switzerland, and Holland as well as England and France. In 1955 he made his first trip to the US and gave talks in New York, Washington, and Cleveland. The few Sufis in the US at that time were mostly elderly mureeds who had been inspired by Murshid when he had been there. By the late 1960s, Pir had students in a number of the Western European countries, but the Sufi Order was growing slowly. The times were not yet right and interest in Sufism itself was starting slowly. In those days, he managed without much organization or support. In fact all he had was a French assistant who ran the office out of her apartment.

Throughout this time Pir continued to live in Suresnes, however it was no longer practical to hold the large Summer Schools there as his father had done. Most of the nearby houses where students had stayed were no longer owned by mureeds. The lecture hall was gone, and the land it had been on had been expropriated for an apartment building. Pir did give classes in the enclosed back porch, looking out on the garden at Fazal Manzil, but it was not very satisfactory for the purpose. He also led small camps in the mountains throughout the 1960s.

Whenever he could manage it, he returned to his cave above Chamonix, where a few determined students began accompanying him, but it meant carrying food and tents high up steep slopes. However, it was a superb location for retreats. He loved to do morning meditations as the sun turned the great peaks golden.

In 1968 Murshid Sam met Pir Vilayat in San Francisco. It was an important meeting. Murshid Sam was just getting started in the role he had long been destined for. He was almost seventy at the time while Vilayat was fifty two and had the recognition which Sam had always lacked. As the successor of Hazrat Inayat Khan, Pir was well along the way to becoming the best known Sufi teacher in the West, although at that point he was mostly unknown in the US.

Sam was very much in tune with the New Age wave that was very cresting at that time. The dances that he began creating were an excellent way to harness the potent New Age energy constructively and he was starting to attract a growing number of students. To the extent that he and Pir Vilayat could work together, they complemented one another, but their energies and personalities were very different. Whereas Vilayat looked every inch the spiritual teacher, the same could not be have been said for Sam. He was not much over five feet tall, had thick glasses and a high voice. The deck of cards life had dealt him seem to have been stacked; he was born the black sheep of a wealthy family who would not even send him to college. However, years of spiritual training in Zen Buddhism and Suffism plus his extensive esoteric knowledge were now very apparent.

Those were very exciting times in the Bay area, and they were certainly exciting for Pir Vilayat as well. The New Age energy was still at its height in the US, but it had barely arrived in Europe. Sam's students organized Pir Vilayat's first US camp the next year. People were attracted by the walks and dances that Sam was creating, which would become an important aspect of the spiritual path for many of them. Vilayat however, did not use them. Instead he led meditations which helped people to reach higher states of consciousness. Even the way they led dhikrs were different. With Sam, they tended to be loud and exuberant, whereas Pir Vilayat insisted that they must be refined.

Psychedelics were giving many people their first experience of expanded consciousness but Pir Vilayat did not trust drugs. He could see what he called the "soul damage" that resulted, and he did not believe that shortcuts to spiritual attainment were useful. He was not one to 'turn on' or 'drop out.' 'Tuning in' was fine, but not by artificial means. He believed in manifesting God in the world, not dropping out of it; while he may have been reclusive, he was not a recluse.

There were even deeper differences. One was the inner connection with the teacher. When Murshid Sam's students said "Murshid" they meant Samuel. By Murshid Pir's students meant Hazrat Inayat Khan. The distinction is important. The connection between mureed and his murshid goes to the heart of the Sufi Path. The disagreement about drugs was a symptom, rather than a cause of these differences. The Order Murshid Sam founded was very different from Pir Vilayat's. More importantly, Sam was clearly not one to respect authority. It would have been difficult for him to work as part of Pir's organization. At times it was even true for him with his own Order, the Ruhaniat.

Despite the two teachers' common devotion to Hazrat Inayat Khan these differences became more and more evident. After several years Pir said the students must make a choice, and the two groups separated. This was very painful for Pir Vilayat and for the students themselves. It took a long time before the scars could heal.

Murshid Sam died in 1971 as the result of a fall; perhaps he had finished his mission, although that seems unlikely. Without him there were difficulties. Moinuddin Jablonski had been named his successor, but he moved to Hawaii, while most of the mureeds lived in California which created difficulties. Murshid Sam had done a fine job in planting the seeds, which continued to blossom after he was gone. His leaders were able to continue what he had started, greatly aided by the dances, which kept on attracting more students.

Over time, more groups were founded by other followers of Hazrat Inayat Khan. They all shared a common dedication to Pir-o-Murshid, but each has evolved in different ways. This is not uncommon among Sufis, where several murshids trained by one teacher may go on to start their own groups, which then branch off from the original tree. In the West the process became more complicated, since it involved formal organizations which had never be used before. An attempt to bridge the differences was started by the Sufi Movement and the Ruhaniat. Their leaders met every year attempting to promote better understanding, and hopefully reunification. In time, the Sufi Order, the Sufi Way, and the Sufi Contact, all of whom were inspired by the teachings of Hazrat Inayat Khan, joined this group which was called the Federation of the Message and began to meet yearly at the Abode of the Message.

A positive result of the divergence has been to provide varied avenues of growth for students with different needs, and thus achieve a greater outreach than the original Sufi Movement could have done. The Sufi Movement stresses continuity and tries to keep the forms that Pir-o-Murshid introduced as unchanged as possible. They have ensured that his teachings are made available in a series of 'Sufi Message' volumes and other publications which have honored his memory with a magnificent building for his tomb in Delhi. From a small start of spiritual walks and dances, the Ruhaniat has created well over a hundred 'Dances of Universal Peace' which Sam's followers have spread around the world. For over forty years these have served as a magnet which continues to attract untold numbers of students to the fold. The Sufi Way experimented with more radical innovation. They offer more varied techniques in addition to those taught by Inayat Khan. Each of these orders gave rise to a number of fine leaders who have continued to spread the teachings further.

Chapter 15
SPREADING THE MESSAGE

Do not try to occupy a position that is not yours. Do not assume that you know when you do not know. Without expending the effort one does not progress, yet our efforts alone can never bring us to the goal. If they could then there would be no place for faith and grace. Dedicate yourself to the service of truth. Your enemy is your best friend in that he reveals to you your weakness. Pain makes the soul sincere. God discovers His perfection in human imperfection. Divinity resides in humanity; it is also the outcome of humanity. Man is divine limitation and God is human perfection.
— PIR VILAYAT INAYAT KHAN, *THE GREAT JOURNEY*

If the measure of a great leader is his ability to inspire, Pir Vilayat had what it took in abundance. Part of the reason was his deep compassion and total dedication to service. These were some of the reasons that we all wanted to serve him. But what he wanted was for us to serve to the Message, not him. His selfless dedication, as well as his compassion and the way he shared his pain, set an example. We could feel the sincerity behind these words:

I have suffered with your suffering and rejoiced with your rejoicings, and I feel that many of you have done the same. Finding a good job is important, but then you come to a point where there is something much more important, and you would like to get a job that really helps the well-being of mankind. You are not so important anymore. You have found something that is worthwhile living and dying for. That's the spirit of the Message — something that makes sense beyond all the sense of anything else in the world.

The trials that he went through, especially after his father's death, then again during the war, followed by all his other losses and finally his struggles to build the Sufi Order seemed to be never ending. His determination, strong will and mastery had no doubt been molded by all the pain he had to endure and the obstacles he had been faced with. He said, "What we cannot endure and pass on to others is a measure of weakness; one becomes great by enduring the unendurable."

He painted his visions with broad brush strokes. But like the faces of the angels, they lacked in fine details. Filling these in was left for others to do. Each new vision entailed overcoming new kinds of opposition. Forces opposed to the light could always find chinks in the knight's armor, or the weakest link in his forces. Naturally the bolder the step forward, the tougher the opposition.

Whatever resisted change went deeply against the grain for Pir Vilayat. Perhaps it was inevitable that some of the challenges came from within the organizations he had created. By their nature organizations can never be as flexible as individuals. There is a tendency for the organization to try and control its founder which as we have seen, also happened to Hazrat Inayat Khan. Pir fiercely resisted control; one way of doing this was to change the plan, which he did often.

Once, when I reminded him that he had just given the group opposite instructions, his response was, "Why, do you mean I can't change my mind?" He did not like to follow his own system, or any system for that matter. I don't believe this was even an intentional thing. His whole being cried for forward movement and change without which there could be no room for creativity.

Immediately after a talk he often asked for a copy of the recording, which he wanted for what he was writing. Strangely he never seemed concerned about what happened to his recordings afterwards. Perhaps since he could no longer change what was on them. This was unfortunate since his talks were often easier to understand than his writings. But nothing could compete with his passion to write. Time and again he laid everything else aside for his creative outlet. As Pir-o-Murshid said, "When creative inspiration is coming through, we are at one with the source of inspiration." Pir liked to go to bed early, but once I found him writing very late, I said, "You can't go on working sixteen hours a day." He seemed to take this as a challenge, and responded, "Oh can't I!"

His written word tended to be too complex. His books were not very popular. I never saw them in a bookstore, let alone in libraries. He must have known this and I wondered how much it mattered to him. A brilliant man whom Pir respected once said of his latest book, "I think there are only four people alive who can understand all of this." I made the mistake of telling it to Pir. He responded with much annoyance, "I don't care." Perhaps he had heard it all too often before.

Maybe he was hinting at something deeper. It could be he was writing for generations to come, for the time when he could be understood. It was through books that he knew his father's teachings. All of what he had learned of the great Sufis came via books. I well understand the importance of passing on his teachings to posterity, as that has become my own mission. However, I believe his most important legacy is in the thousands of students whom he helped transform, and the many fine teachers he trained, who continue to spread his legacy worldwide. Already the ten thousand workers Inayat Khan predicted have been inspired by the Message which his son brought.

For Pir, it was this inspiration that counted; if this meant that orderly procedures had to be sacrificed, then so be it. One would hardly call him a good administrator. In general, he left administration to those he selected. Since he was a fine judge of people, he was able to select good administrators when they were available. He made decisions with certainty and just as easily reversed them, sometimes for no apparent reason. He could see the truth in two opposing points of view. On occasion he made far reaching decisions based on what seemed to be momentary inspiration. What helped was the power of his intuition and his ability to apprehend the higher purpose of things.

Whether it was an inspiration, or a project long held dear to his heart, his enthusiasm could be infectious. To the conventional mind some of his schemes might seem fantastic. Building a temple of all religions in his backyard was one such example. Certainly it appeared that way to the municipal authorities in Suresnes who turned it down. Pir's inventive genius then presented it as a memorial to Noor-un-Nisa who grew up here and was a local resistance heroine. Framed that way, it was hard for them to oppose it.

Many consider his greatest inspiration was the alchemical retreat which became the centerpiece of his work. Retreats had long been part of the Sufi tradition. In the thirteenth Century Shahabuddin Suhrawardi had given detailed instructions for a forty day retreat with fasting and continuous dhikr, much as Pir himself had done. Pir however, had taken it much further by combining it with techniques from other traditions, and integrating them with the *Ars Regia* — The Royal Art, which scholars believe may have been taught to the Christians by the Sufis in Spain. Pir's creative genius enabled him to integrate these processes with the traditional dhikr and wazifa, creating a new format.

By the early 1970s, he had the components of each stage of the structure ready for assembly, but had not yet put them in place. Whereas his father had taught his ideas methodically, Pir Vilayat's way was to build down; he was a high climber who liked to dwell on the upper stories with a wide view. From there he found it easier to reach down for the pieces just as he needed them, rather than lifting them up from below and cementing them permanently in place.

To understand how Pir Vilayat evolved the retreat format it is interesting to compare the process in the early days to what it was to become. The basics were all there by the time he first brought it to the US. The process involved: dissolving, distilling, separating and fixing, and required passing through a dark night and a rebirth. The ultimate aim was to transmute the dross of one's lower nature into the gold of an evolved being. To do this he employed breath, light, mantra, and dhikr, but it took time before they were organized into the retreat form that they were to become. His inspiration would be a way these could be integrated into a coherent whole. In this, his genius for synthesis was evident. Once the form was together, he could also start training retreat guides to use it. It was all an experiment and he loved to experiment. When he felt it was finished, he could then move on to something else, in this he was very much a part of the evolving New Age.

The alchemical retreat exemplified what he aspired to do. The purpose of his retreats was transformation, by which he meant "learning to shift from the earthly to the divine point of view," or "integrating one's individual identity and personal vantage point with that of the

Divine." It involves working with different energies along with the breath, and requires determination, endurance and patience. One could expect pain and difficulties. It also requires surrender and trust. The end result would hopefully be what he called "Awakening in Life," and the transformation of ones leaden dross into gold.

There was always the risk that such a system, could turn into an impediment. The alchemical format was just one possible way to do a retreat. It could never be right for everyone. A person on retreat might need to concentrate on just one stage or not follow the prescribed order at all. Pir Vilayat knew this; he rarely followed the entire six stages himself. Others doing or leading retreats might not realize this. It is worthwhile to remember that there are so many possible ways to do a retreat, which range from repeating koans or staring at a blank wall, to watching the breath or chanting a mantra. Many of these were right for the people doing them. Over the years a great variety of seekers from many traditions have done this form of retreat and have been transformed. These included a number of Christian ministers, a few even reported having their first mystical experiences. Hopefully the day will come when people from other traditions and on different spiritual paths, will employ some of retreat practices based on Pir Vilayat's inspirations.

Pir's whole life was devoted to service. He longed for the solace of the mountains and the quiet of a cave, but all too often his days were filled with seminars, and organizational matters. He traveled with a beggar's bowl to support the Hope Project, but never asked for himself or his organization. Year after year he packed his schedule full, crossing the Atlantic, sometimes for only a few days. The constant jet lag and fatigue took a growing toll on him. I often wondered just how much of our pain did Pir Vilayat take on. Naturally this was something he would never speak of and I never heard a word of complaint, but he did say that the Murshid actually does share some of the mureed's karma.

One might think that he was comfortable in his role as head of a large organization with centers in dozens of countries. Actually, it was the heaviest cross of the many he had to bear. He was totally dedicated to his mission, but it demanded all his strength and then some. After long days of talking and giving initiations he would be so tired that he could barely walk. He was frequently called upon to settle disputes among his helpers or make what he believed were the critical decisions required of the Pir which proved unpopular. The split that occurred with the Ruhaniat was a painful case of what happened when others could not accept his decisions. This was no doubt an example of why his mother had tried so hard to prevent him following in his father's footsteps.

In his first few years in the US, Pir Vilayat had attracted a number of highly evolved mureeds with great leadership potential whom he could train quite quickly. They began forming new centers and could then initiate many more students, until there were over seventy-five centers and study groups just in the US. Over twenty-five years he initiated more than five thousand mureeds in this country, and in time close to the same number again worldwide, including students in Europe, Canada, Mexico, Chile, New Zealand and Australia. He also founded Omega Institute, which became the largest spiritual retreat and seminar center on the East Coast. It had started at the Abode and was moved to Rhinebeck, NY by its director, Stephen Rechtschaffen.

As the numbers of students grew, there was a need for more teachers and centers. Pir Vilayat's solution was to give leaders training at the Abode summer camp, assisted by one or two of the leaders he had already trained. Each one had different strengths which they expressed in their own ways. However, increasingly his presence was so large, there was not enough space for him and other leaders under one roof. As a consequence, many of them moved out in different directions, where they had the freedom to teach in their own way. They clearly needed the freedom he himself required. Personally I regretted this, knowing how much each had to offer, but on the plus side, it did make a greater variety of teachings available. I wonder whether Pir knew this and unconsciously pushed them out of the nest. They have been able to spread Murshid's teachings throughout Europe, and then beyond.

The European camps required translation, but Pir Vilayat was understandably very hard to translate. His solution was to translate all three languages himself, one after the other. He told me that this was damaging his brain and he was going to stop, but of course he didn't. He would translate one idea into French and then German, more or less. Sometimes a thought would continue on in the next language, so that the group at the end might get the middle and the conclusion, but would have to guess at how it had started, but no one seemed to mind. Of course some of his ideas were beyond words in any language and we all loved just being there with him. His tendency was to push all limits, including his own. His son Zia said that he had learned much of his own French listening to his father doing his own translations at the Alps camp.

In all the time I knew him, Pir Vilayat never once listened to a radio or watched a TV. Instead he tuned into higher channels where he believed much of the future was being determined. He had a poor opinion of much of the media and a distrust of TV interviews from personal experience. One of the first ones he did had been a set up. The interviewer asked him tricky questions on a live broadcast. Eventually he came to realize how useful the media could be. An hour long documentary on German national TV, shot at the Abode and in California brought many enthusiastic new students to him. I began to video tape him, which he graciously put up with. He always found the bright lights inspiring, no doubt because he so loved light.

When Inayat Khan came to the West, he had to overcome many difficulties himself. When he first started giving talks, it was as a Sufi raised in Islam He soon discovered his audiences did not know what Sufism was, and had little interest in learning about it, let alone any thing about Islam. Many were Theosophists and were hoping to find a master from the East. He was forced to rely on the core Sufi wisdom minus the traditional terminology and on the universal truths and mystical wisdom underlying all faiths.

The Sufi tradition in India, and especially that practiced by Murshid's lineage, was more tolerant than most practiced in the Arab lands. Living in close proximity to Hindus as well as Jains and Sikhs, Sufis throughout Southern Asia had developed an open-minded acceptance of different creeds and customs. Coming from such a background, Inayat's genius enabled him to adapt the traditional teachings to Western audiences without losing sight of its underlying truths. Thus, he was able to modernize the ancient wisdom. What he taught was in many ways a modern version of the Perennial Philosophy adding his father's and his own deep insights.

Pir was able to take this process much further than what his father could manage. He introduced practices from other traditions as well as traditional forms such as retreats, wazifas, and the dhikr, which Murshid had not taught publicly. He also expanded and elucidated what his father had taught. However, his growing fame exposed him to criticism from a growing number of sources. As time went on, more Sufi teachers came to the West but he like his father had to suffer the tribulations of being the first.

Western members of the "Traditionalist" school such as Frithjof Schuon said that modern approaches dilute the value of traditional Sufism. Once a Sufi sheikh from Jerusalem came to visit the Abode. His translator explained that it was difficult for them to communicate. The real problem was not language, but bridging the gap between their world views, one bounded by the walls of a small divided city, the other cosmic. Actually Pir Vilayat managed to infuse the form with new vitality and show how Suffism applied to modern life in the Age of Materialism.

Orthodox Muslims have long been suspicious of Sufis. There is also a lack of innovation among traditional Sufis. Murshid was criticized for not using the traditional prayers. Pir Vilayat was criticized for revealing "secret" teachings. Actually, the practices he taught could be found in books which were unknown in the West and not much known in the East anymore. He was part of a whole trend that has been changing our ideas on what should and should not be kept secret.

As the case of Al Hallaj, who was crucified for heresy shows, it is often the fate of great beings to be misunderstood. This is true among all religions, but especially in the case of dervishes. Typically these great beings were not willing to defend themselves against false accusations. Pir Vilayat himself would never deign to publicly argue with his attackers or those who defamed him.

Pir's concern was never with doctrines or forms; what he strove for was to help his students gain realization. What both he and his father did was to broaden and deepen our understanding of the meaning of the Sufi path. In this they proved themselves to be great spiritual innovators, as well as worthy successors to the Sufi masters of the past. Over the years Pir Vilayat's books, the large number of his students, and his many other accomplishments, spoke louder than any words could do for him.

He was very excited about new trends and developments, but was very concerned with the direction events were taking. He was quite pessimistic about the future if such negative trends continued. Sometimes he was able to get glimpses of what lay ahead. For example he felt sure that there would be destructive earthquakes in California although he had been wrong about the timing. He also admitted that he was overly pessimistic at times, as he had been about the Three Mile Island reactor accident which he correctly predicted, but over estimated its severity. He foresaw a time of cleansing for the planet which would be triggered by violent upheavals of earth and fire as well as great storms, but he said he had no idea when. He believed that our materialistic civilization was reaching its conclusion and believed a new start was required.

In his final months, Taj and Pir's younger son Mirza stayed in Fazal Mazil with him. Here is something she wrote about those times:

> It took weeks after Pir Vilayat's first stroke for him to recover his ability to speak and communicate his ideas. Gradually, he developed a system of communication where he would dictate his thoughts and have them read back to him. Try to imagine, if you will, the difficulty of keeping the sequence of entire paragraphs clearly in his mind as he listened to what was dictated back to him and then made revisions.
>
> It was a tedious process, but one that he never seemed to get tired of. He often dozed off into sleeping episodes, yet upon waking he would always say, "Now, where were we?" Then he would begin again immediately. This went on for days and weeks. He worked intensely on several articles, some of which were released before his death in issues of Keeping in Touch.
>
> One day he said that he would like to write an article on meditation with me, that we would each write a portion of it. At first, I didn't think he was serious, so I tried to delay it several days. I thought he was just trying to keep me busy.... When he finished

his portion I hadn't even started mine. Every time he asked how my part was coming along, I responded with some excuse. But he continued to bring it up, until I started feeling guilty and finally began to write down a few thoughts.

Then of course, I would have to read back to him what I had written and he would ponder what I had said. His eyes would light up at certain points, such as the phrase "God becomes man so that man can become God." I never found the source of that quote. I must have read my portion of this article to him twenty times, sometimes nearly screaming in his ear because of his hearing loss. I thought the other family members in the house surely must be sick of it, but he never appeared tired of hearing it. He seemed happy to see the two poles of meditation spoken about together.

I remember that time now with so much tenderness. I feel grateful in those last days, even under such difficult circumstances, to have had the joy of sharing deeply our inner thoughts and experiences as we had for over thirty-five years. In some way, this Keeping in Touch is a testament to our ongoing dialogue: the conversation we started when we first met and which continued until he was not longer able to speak.

This story beautifully illustrates how important were the roles of the transcendent and the immanent in his life, as well as all that Taj continued to bring to him herself. He chose to concentrate on what he still wanted to do; there would always be more. He kept on trying to plant seeds for the future, although naturally these were not likely to bloom in his lifetime. However, towards the end, as his health was failing, it seemed that his regrets began to loom larger in his mind than all his accomplishments. In the final years of his life, he was increasingly bedridden and only able to walk with crutches at best, however he still managed to keep on writing his Keeping In Touch newsletters.

Now his son could hopefully take up his part in the revolution in thinking that was to bring down ossified structures and beliefs, allow the feminine to take its own rightful place, and strive for understanding among different religions. As forces of reaction attempt to turn back the clock and fend off the threat of change and globalization, hopefully a modernized Sufism can provide an alternative to conservative Islam and give support to those forces within it which are striving to modernize it.

This is a task that Pir Vilayat left for his successors to undertake.

I think Pir's fame meant little to him, except perhaps in the way it helped him to reach more people, and thus better fulfill his mission. It also enabled him to meet many of the thinkers on the forefront of evolution. In this way, he could better act as a catalyst and plant seminal ideas where they could be most effective.

I suspect that Pir sometimes doubted how well he had done in carrying out the task entrusted to him by his father. Could that explain why he always had to do more? Actually, there is no doubt that his father would have been deeply satisfied to see how the seeds he planted have grown into a mighty tree, an oak with many branches. How could Murshid not have been pleased by how much his son had accomplished in his absence, and despite almost insurmountable obstacles?

Even though Pir and Taj were to move apart, their spiritual connection was permanent and continued on this plane until his dying breath. She and their son Mirza were there when he breathed his last and went to India along with Zia to oversee his burial, not far from where his own father was buried. Pir Vilayat had the satisfaction of knowing that he was leaving his legacy in good hands. Speaking of his son Zia he said, "He is more intelligent and a greater mystic than I am." I believe he was not saying this just as a proud father. He was also clear that Zia would do things his own way.

Thinking back about his life Pir Vilayat wrote, "My teachings can be considered as variations on a theme, and the theme is Murshid's. It has taken me all these years to appreciate the importance of the Message in all its vastness, and particularly to see its relevance for our time. When I was younger, the Message was just a word to me."

He wrote: "Unless an organism, and this applies to organizations, improves and perfects itself, it eventually finds itself redundant in the scheme of things, it may stagnate for some time, then perish." He was constantly looking ahead, he said, "Spirituality needs to be updated" He spoke of a new "space age spirituality," which could help people experience further dimensions of reality. Based on how often he spoke of the importance of remembering our solar and galactic inheritance, it appeared he looked forward to start exploring the galaxy.

He said, "We are all part of the evolution of humanity. We might be the leading edge in bringing about the purpose of the Universe. The more we evolve, the more universal our sense of identity." With his help we became increasingly aware of it. His mottos were "Always a little further" and "What if?"

Some of his last words were, "I will not be able to give seminars anymore, but I am working on seven levels of light, and I will be with our mureeds that way." He passed away on June 17th, 2004. At the Abode people saw a rainbow in the sky. His body first rested in state in the Universel, in the garden of Fazal Manzil that he loved so well. Finally he was buried near his father's tomb in India.

It is too soon to judge Pir Vilayat's place in history, and doubly difficult since his main impact was on those that he inspired directly. Since he met some of the foremost thinkers and spiritual leaders of our time, and was himself one of them, his impact on their thinking may well have been significant, but much of it is not easily documented. A better way of judging this is by how much he was loved, his effect on his students, and what they have gone on to accomplish.

His spirit lives on now, led by his son, who is building his own edifice on the framework his father and grandfather built, and continues to build it higher. No doubt Pir was correct in believing that he had left the work in good hands.

NOTES

Chapter 1: The Early Years
Pir Vilayat Inayat Khan, "The Great Journey," *The Classic Pir Vilayat*,
    CD vol. 2, track 1. from tape (1975.)
Jodjana, Raden Ayou, "Autobiography,'" *A Pearl In Wine*, Omega
    Publications, New Lebanon, (2001).
PVK, "Memories of My Life," *Heart & Wings* supplement
    (May 1986)
PVK, *The Message In Our Time*, Omega Publications,
    New Lebanon: (2004) p. 4.
PVK, *The Call of the Dervish*. Omega Publications, 1981, Chapter 15.
Claire Harper and David Harper, *We Rubies Four*,
    Omega Publications, New Lebanon: (2011).
Hidayat Inayat Khan, "Once Upon a Time",
    The Message magazine (January 1984).
PVK, *Heart & Wings*, memorial edition, New Lebanon (2004).
PVK, "In His Own Words," *The Message* magazine ,
    (March/April1983).
PVK, *Heart & Wings* (September/October 1985), pp. 7-8.
Elise Guillaume-Schamhart and Munira van Voorst van Beest,
    Eds., *Biography of Pir-o-Murshid Inayat Khan*,
    The Hague, East-West Publications Fonds BV, (1979).
"Fatha Engel": *Biography, Autobiography, Journal and Anecdotes:
    Biographical Sketches of Principal Workers*. Retrieved from
    http://wahiduddin.net/mv2/bio/Sketches.htm
Wil van Beek, *Hazrat Inayat Khan*, New York, Vantage Press, 1983.

CHAPTER 2: LIFE WITHOUT MURSHID
PVK, "The Great Journey" *The Classic Pir Vilayat*, CD vol. 2, track 1.
PVK, *That Which Transpires Behind That Which Appears*,
    Omega Press, New Lebanon, NY (1994).
Zia Inayat-Khan, *"A Hybrid Sufi Order at the Crossroads of
    Modernity."* PhD dissertation, Duke University, (2006).
Claire Harper, *We Rubies Four.*
Hidayat Inayat Khan, "Once Upon a Time", *The Message* magazine
    (Jan 1984).

PVK, *Reflections at the Abode* (2001) Unpublished manuscript.

PVK, "Memories of My Life". Unpublished manuscript.

Jean Overton Fuller, *Noor-un-Nisa Inayat Khan: Madeleine,*
        London: East West Publications, (1988).

Claire Harper *We Rubies Four.*

PVK, *Reflections at the Abode* (2001). Unpublished manuscript.

PVK, *Call of the Dervish*, Chap 15.

PVK, "Memories of My Life".

PVK et al, *Leaders' Manual,*
        Sufi Order International, p. 34 restricted circulation.

Rob Baker and Gray Henry, *Merton & Sufism: The Untold Story,*
        Louisville: Fons Vitae, (1999).

Chapter 3: The War Years and After

PVK, "The Great Journey" *The Classic Pir Vilayat*, CD vol. 2, track 1.

PVK, *Heart & Wings*, memorial edition, New Lebanon (2004).

PVK, "Memories of My Life".

Claire Harper *We Rubies Four.*

Jean Overton Fuller, *Noor-un-Nisa Inayat Khan.*

Vilayat Inayat Khan, *Awakening: A Sufi Experience*, New York.
        J.P. Tarcher/Putnam, (1999) p. 211.

PVK, *Heart & Wings*, memorial edition (2004).

PVK, *The Message* magazine, "Memories of Flight", (Dec 1978).

PVK, *Reflections at the Abode* (2001).

PVK, "Dreaming Images," *The Message* magazine (May/June 1984).

PVK, "Memories of My Life".

PVK, *The Message* magazine (December 1978).

PVK, *Heart & Wings* (May 1986).

PVK, *The Message* magazine, "Remarks on Music" (April 1979).

Mary Inayat Khan interview by Devi Tide, private communication.

Chapter 4: Rishis and Hermits

PVK, "The Great Journey," CD.

PVK, *Heart & Wings*, memorial edition (2004).

PVK, *Call of the Dervish*,   Omega Publications (1981) Chap 15.

PVK, "Attunement To The Spiritual Hierarchy"
        The Message magazine (February 1980).

PVK, *The Message* magazine (November 1979).
Leaders' Manual, vol. 2.
PVK, *The Message* magazine (June/July 1980).

Chapter 5: A Dervish in the Making
PVK, "The Great Journey," CD.
Pir Rashid Interview by Prof Scott Kugel, private communication.
PVK, *Reflections at the Abode* (2001).
PVK, *Toward The One*, New York, Harper & Row: (1974).
PVK, *The Message* magazine(June 1976).
        Leaders' Manual, Vol. 2, p. 173. Sufi Order.
PVK, *Call of the Dervish*, Omega Publications, 1981

CHAPTER 6: PILGRIMAGES AND RETREATS
PVK, "The Great Journey," CD.
PVK, *The Message* magazine (October 1978).

CHAPTER 7: RIDING THE NEW AGE WAVE
PVK, "The Great Journey," CD.
PVK, *The Call of Thee Dervish*, Sufi Order Publications ,
        Sante Fe, NM (1991).
PVK, "Memories of My Life".

CHAPTER 8: THE MUSIC OF LIFE
Hazrat Inayat Khan, *The Music of Life*,
        Omega Press, New Lebanon (1983).
PVK, "Creativity", *The Message* magazine (July- August 1982).
PVK, Inayat Khan, *Toward the One*, Harper Colophon *(1974).*
PVK, vol. 5, no. 4 (April 1979).
PVK, *Call of the Dervish*,   Omega Publications (1981) pp. 40-42.
Sharam Nazari "A Tree With A Hundred Flowers," Songs of Rumi.
PVK, *The Message* magazine (April 1979).
PVK, "Memories of My Life".

CHAPTER 9: THE MASTERS
PVK, "The Great Journey," CD.

PVK, *The Message* magazine (October 1977).

CHAPTER 10: ANGELS AND JINNS
PVK, "The Great Journey," CD.
PVK, *Toward The One*.
PVK, *The Message in Our Time*, p 227.
PVK, *Classic Pir Vilayat*, vol. 5. tape and CD.
PVK, *The Message* magazine (September 1979).
PVK, *Classic Pir Vilayat*, vol. 2, tracks 3-8. Tape and CD.

CHAPTER 11: THE SPIRITUAL GOVERNMENT OF THE WORLD
PVK, "The Great Journey," CD.
PVK, *The Message* magazine "Attunement to The Spiritual Hierarchy", (Feb 1980).
Taj Inayat, *The Message* magazine, "The Spirit Hierarchy", (June 1977).
HIK, *Music of Life*, Omega Press New Lebanon NY, (1983) pp. 101
PVK, Elements, cassette tape. (1994)
PVK, *The Message* magazine (June/July 1980), pp. 24-25.
PVK, *Classic Pir Vilayat*, vol. 2. CD.
PVK, *The Message* magazine (September 1979).
PVK, *Classic Pir Vilayat*, Vols. 2-9. tape and CD.
PVK, *The Message* magazine (January 1984).
PVK, *Classic Pir Vilayat*, vols. 2-9. tapes and CD.
Wasserstein, Bernard, *The Secret Lives of Trebitsch Lincoln* New Haven: Yale University Press, (1988).

CHAPTER 12: A SPIRITUAL GIANT
PVK, "The Great Journey," CD.
PVK, *Call of the Dervish*, pp. 40-41, pp. 111-112.
PVK, "Man of God", Nature of The Prophet , tape & CD.
PVK, *That Which Transpires Behind That Which Appears*, Omega Pub
PVK, *Toward the One*, p. 624.
PVK, *Call of the Dervish*, p. 117,- 112.
PVK, "Becoming the Holy Warrior",
    Emergence vol. 1, no. 2 (Spring 1988)
Hazrat Inayat Khan, *The Soul's Journey*, p. 122.
PVK, *Awakening*, pp. 29-30.

Chapter 13: The Task of the Guide
PVK, "The Great Journey," CD.
Hazrat Inayat Khan, *The Sufi Message of Hazrat Inayat Khan Volume I*, - I – 3.
PVK, "Memories of My Life".
Hazrat Inayat Khan, *Sangithas,* Restricted circulation.
PVK, *Toward the One.*
PVK, tape wazifa "It Is." Undated
Initiation, Sufi Order International, Unpublished (1981).
The Message magazine (January 1978).
"The Guru Syndrome," *Keeping in Touch*, no. 30. Retrieved from
    http://centrum-universel.com/KIT_E/E030.htm.
Hazrat Inayat Khan, *Toward the One*, p. 454.

Chapter 14: The Parting of the Ways
PVK, "The Great Journey," CD.
PVK, *Heart & Wings.*
PVK, *The Message* magazine "Declaration" drug policy, (July 1977)
PVK, "Memories of My Life".
Zia Inayat-Khan, "*Hybrid Sufi Order*", PhD dissertation.

Chapter 15: Spreading The Message
PVK, "The Great Journey" CD.
Frithjof Schuon, *The Transcendent Unity of Religions,*
    Quest Books (1984).
PVK, *The Message* magazine (June 1976).
PVK, "Curriculum of the Sufi Order", *Keeping In Touch*, no. 120.
    Retrieved from http://www.centrum-universel.com/EKIT.pdf
Taj Inayat, Personal communication. 2017.

ABOUT THE AUTHOR

MIKHAIL HOROWITZ was a student and confidant of Pir Vilayat for many years. As a recording engineer his work enabled him to accompany him to his retreats and seminars around the world. Before this he spent years studying with Hindu, Buddhist and Christian masters. He is the author of the forth coming book *Travels with the Masters - Adventures in the New Age,* a memoir of his mystical search and his studies with Pir Vilayat and other great masters of our times.

Made in the USA
Columbia, SC
14 January 2019